Praise for

How to Human

"Did politicians make us all forget how to human? Should we point the finger at social media? Is the economy to blame? I'm not sure. But I am certain that Carlos has created an antidote to what ails us. Clear, hopeful, and full of truth, he has once again charted a path to a better world."

—Jon Acuff, *New York Times* bestselling author of *Soundtracks: The Surprising Solution to Overthinking*

"Wherever Carlos appears, whether on social media, in his books, or in person as a friend, he shows us how to be a good human. Now we have his stories and God-given heart for humanity in *How to Human*, and I couldn't be more excited. Carlos continually reminds me that while there's so much suffering in this life, there's so much goodness too. He helps us see the people around us, remembering that everyday moments are something sacred. Carlos lives like Jesus and reflects our Savior as He deals hope to a world that desperately needs it. This book is for anyone who wants that too—it's a must-read!"

—Lysa TerKeurst, #1 *New York Times* bestselling author and president of Proverbs 31 Ministries

"Carlos lives it first, writes it second. This is one of his superpowers. He faces life's challenges head-on and then invites us to do the same. *How To Human* is inspiring, challenging, inviting, and hopeful. This is the book we need right now."

—Annie F. Downs, *New York Times* bestselling author of *That Sounds Fun: The Joys of Being an Amateur, the Power of Falling in Love, and Why You Need a Hobby*

"Carlos exemplifies how to see people, love people, and make people feel truly alive, with simplicity and pure kindness. If the media and your endless scrolling have you feeling weary, divided, and left with less hope in humanity, let Carlos show you these simple yet profound steps to strengthening your own soul so you can love others well and infuse your world with hope. *How to Human* will give you the tools you need to take the first small yet significant step into radical kindness and becoming who you were created to be."

—Levi Lusko, author of *The Marriage Devotional: 52 Days to Strengthen the Soul of Your Marriage*

"In a world full of chaos, division, confusion, pain, and suffering, Carlos has given us a gift of hope in *How to Human*. This book is down-to-earth, raw, vulnerable, hilarious, and timely. If we apply the wisdom contained in these pages, we will find the purpose, love, hope, joy, compassion, and peace we all long for."

—Christine Caine, founder of A21 and Propel Women

how to human

how
to
human

· · ·

THREE WAYS to SHARE LIFE
BEYOND WHAT DISTRACTS, DIVIDES,
and DISCONNECTS US

CARLOS WHITTAKER

FOREWORD BY SHARON McMAHON

WATERBROOK

Details in some anecdotes and stories have been changed to protect
the identities of the persons involved.

Copyright © 2023 by Carlos Enrique Whittaker
Foreword copyright © 2023 by Sharon McMahon

All rights reserved.

Published in the United States by WaterBrook, an imprint of Random House,
a division of Penguin Random House LLC.

WATERBROOK® and its deer colophon are registered trademarks
of Penguin Random House LLC.

Trade Paperback ISBN 978-0-52565-402-5
Ebook ISBN 978-0-52565-403-2

The Cataloging-in-Publication Data is on file with the Library of Congress.

PRINTED IN THE UNITED STATES OF AMERICA ON ACID-FREE PAPER

waterbrookmultnomah.com

2 4 6 8 9 7 5 3 1

First Edition

SPECIAL SALES
Most WaterBrook books are available at special quantity discounts when purchased
in bulk by corporations, organizations, and special-interest groups. Custom
imprinting or excerpting can also be done to fit special needs. For information,
please email specialmarketscms@penguinrandomhouse.com.

Seanna, this book is dedicated to you.
I'm so lucky to have had the privilege of being your dad
and watching you be human for eighteen years.
Now the world gets a front-row seat—
go show it what you've taught me.

FOREWORD

E ven before Carlos Whittaker and I were friends, I admired him. I remember perusing his Instagram account for the first time and thinking that this person was way out of my friend league—someone as cool as him would never be friends with someone as pedestrian as me. He had almost a hundred thousand followers, people who obviously agreed with my conclusion: He is *cool*. I couldn't help comparing myself to him.

After all, Carlos wrote books. I did not.

Carlos flew all over the country speaking to people. I did not.

Carlos had followers. I did not.

Carlos was the kind of person who hugged strangers on the street. I avoided eye contact with people in public.

So, imagine my surprise in 2020 when Carlos mentioned my name to his followers. In our first interaction, I replied with, "I am in tears. Thank you so much. I truly admire you and am so honored you would mention me." He wrote back, "You are a gift, Sharon! 10,000 thank yous for everything you put out there."

And with that, a friendship was born. The next day, we were talking about Bigfoot. A few days later, it was whale barnacles and Black Lives Matter. Soon, it was crunchy peanut butter and Internet misinformation, theocracy, injured owls, Christmas inflatables, nesting birds, and January 6.

Turns out, now that I've gotten to know him, Carlos isn't as good as I thought he was. He's *better*. Who you see in front of the screen really is the person he is behind the screen. The man on the pages you're about to read isn't hiding behind a facade of relatability; it's who he *is*. Flawed, sure, as we all are, but Carlos is one of the few people I know who would get on a plane within an hour if I needed him. His unique ability to encourage and uplift empowers him to look incredible adversity in the face and tell it to move aside, even though his eyes may be teary and his voice might crack.

In early 2022, Carlos took his family on a vacation to Hawaii, and they booked a whale-watching excursion. They motored out into the impossibly blue water, the boat full of people gazing hopefully at the horizon. When a humpback whale surfaced to breathe nearby, the boat, motor cut, floated near it. Passengers murmured with quiet excitement, "Ooh, there it is! Shh."

At that moment, the whale hurled itself out of the water, more vertical than should be possible, and then landed with an enormous splash. In the video Carlos was taking, he is screaming with joy, awestruck. The humpback rewarded the passengers by leaping out of the water again and again, coming down with tremendous force, rocking the boat with waves.

All the while, Carlos yelled with delight. Eventually he turned the camera on himself. You can see his mouth hanging open, his eyebrows nearly reaching the top of his bald head, his stunned expression showing the most genuine reaction one could have to this majesty of nature.

Suddenly, he flipped the camera back around and he shouted,

"Sharon, this is for you!" The whale came down again with a mighty slap on the blue surface, just feet away from the boat.

And my friends, *that* is Carlos. A man who thinks of others in a moment of delight and wants to share it with them. A man who dedicates a whale breach in your honor. A man whose giant eyes tear up on an airplane when he reads his DMs and who can make others tear up with his words on stage.

"Don't stand on issues. Walk with people," Carlos repeats to his Instafamilia and in this book. Carlos walks that walk. He walks it in the whale breaches and the prison visiting rooms, in the hospital room of his daughter and in the pages you're about to read.

I hope you will enjoy this book. But more than that, I hope you will enjoy getting to know my friend. He is exactly who we need, today and every day, as we all learn together how to human.

—Sharon McMahon
@SharonSaysSo

CONTENTS

SECTION 3 • **free**

INTRODUCTION

It was 1985. I was in fifth grade and wore a parted Afro that would have made Arnold from *Diff'rent Strokes* jealous. I remember all my friends wanted to touch it. And I remember that not being weird.

I mean, who could blame them? Such a soft, perfectly round Afro. After all, I was the only friend in my friend group who had a perfectly rounded sphere on my head. All my other friends were White. They didn't have hair like mine. I secretly wished I had their hair, but I don't remember the girl I had a crush on at the time, Amber, touching *their* hair. She only touched mine, so at least that was a plus.

My barber was a guy by the name of Curtis. Curtis cut hair at Northlake Mall in Decatur, Georgia. I don't remember much about him other than the fact that he smelled so good. Like, almost *too* good, if that makes sense. Man, he smelled good. The whole barbershop smelled like Curtis. My mom didn't think it smelled good, but I did. Curtis smelled like what a third-grade boy thought a man should smell like. That smell always meant that my baby 'fro was about to get sculpted, and it wouldn't take Curtis long. Probably only about ten minutes, but I loved those ten minutes.

Curtis would wrap my neck in a towel and sweep that plastic cape up into the wind from the corner fan, letting it cover me. I loved the way the cape sounded like a whip cracking when it opened and the way it would slowly settle down against me like a parachute landing. It felt so majestic. He would spin me in the chair toward the mirror and start the trimmer. I'd close my eyes and almost fall asleep every time. *Amazing.**

So, I'm sitting there one day getting my hair cut with my eyes closed. Curtis was talking to my mom about some boring grown-up stuff. Suddenly we heard shouting coming from outside the shop. It wasn't shouting like *angry* shouting. It was different. Scarier. It was a woman, whose shouting was getting louder. Nobody shouted back at her—somehow that was scariest of all.

As the trimmer buzzed past my left ear, I opened my eyes. I'll never forget what I saw. A man came running past the front window of the shop. Running *so* fast. He was carrying a kid who was even younger than me, probably just four or five years old. The kid wasn't screaming, but he was bouncing with every step the man took as he sprinted past the front window. The man wasn't screaming, but the woman's screams were getting even louder—the lady who was chasing him.

And then *whoosh!*

Another person went sprinting by the door. Then another and another. Now more people were screaming, not just the woman. Then, in what seemed like slow motion, Curtis

---

* Being totally transparent here, and seeing that I am completely lacking the ability to grow *any* hair at this point in my life, I'm enjoying *way* too much this opportunity to reminisce about when I actually could get a haircut. (Is it still that good, guys?)

dropped his clippers on the ground and sprinted out the door. He'd been halfway from the front of my 'fro to the back when he dropped them, still switched on. They were vibrating on the floor of the barbershop as I sat there.

My mom started yelling at me. *"¡Carlitos, ven aquí! ¡Ven aquí!"* ("Carlos, come here! Come here!")

I was scared 'cause the woman screaming was clearly scared and everything felt so chaotic. I jumped off the chair and ran over to my mom. She held me tighter than normal. There was more chaos outside the front window of the barbershop as I saw more people running past.

"Carlitos, I think someone's baby got kidnapped," my mom said.

We sat in the barbershop holding each other for a few minutes. When all the screaming stopped, my mom and I walked out the front door. We went down the huge hallway on the second level of the mall, moving toward the source of the commotion. There was a police car and sirens in the background and probably fifty or so people gathered at the end of the mall hallway.

As we got closer, I saw Curtis! He was talking to one of the police officers. There were roughly seven other men talking to police officers too. I remember them so clearly. One was a heavyset older Black man. He was breathing deeply, and he kind of looked like my uncle Denicio. He had a bunch of moles on his neck and seemed to be talking more with his eyes than his mouth. Then there were two younger men who looked like brothers. They were White and really skinny like me. They might have been eighteen years old, and they weren't breathing that hard. But they talked one hundred miles an hour, like they were almost giddy, gesturing with their hands. They wore tank tops and jean shorts and looked a bit like the boys who picked on me at school. Then there was a rich guy. I say "rich guy" only because he wore what my friend Billy's dad wore. And Billy was rich. He lived over on Windfield Circle, where all my rich friends lived. *Must be rich,* I thought. Curtis was talking, loudly. A police officer wrote down everything he said.

And then I saw the mom. It had to be her because she stood there sobbing and holding the little kid the running man had been carrying. Did they catch him? *There was no way Curtis caught him,* I thought. *I saw Curtis run out the door. No way Curtis caught him. Curtis had to have caught up after the faster guys caught the bad guy.* As I looked around, though, I didn't see any sign of the bad guy who took the kid. Maybe they had him cuffed and in the police car.

"I sure hope Curtis is gonna finish your hair, Carlitos, 'cause it's looking lumpy," my mom said, laughing and hugging me. I felt so safe when she hugged me like that. And I felt even safer than normal in that moment.

A few minutes later, Curtis came walking toward us. "We got him. We got the @#*%$. And I gave it to him," he said. "I really gave it to him."

Even in fifth grade, I knew what that meant. *Good for Curtis.* I would have punched him too. "C'mon, kid. Let's finish taming that mane," Curtis said as we walked back to the barbershop laughing about how out of shape he was.

• • •

I don't remember much else about that day, but my fifth-grade brain did hang on to one takeaway from the experience. As I've thought about that scene many times since, I realize that when Curtis saw the other men running by, he didn't stop to think.

He saw two skinny White kids. A rich guy. A Black man that looked like my uncle.

Curtis didn't ask them what they were doing. He didn't hesitate. He dropped the trimmer and ran. Curtis didn't ask them where they lived. He just ran. Curtis didn't ask them who they voted for. He just ran. Why? Did he think about it and research if he should run after the bad guy or not? No. He just did what he did. Why? Because that's what was inside him. And that's what was inside all those other guys too. They came together to do the right thing. As humans.

They didn't have a meeting or form a committee or hold a conversation to try to figure out what the right thing was. They knew. And they ran. Because deep down, even if they didn't realize it, that's what humans were created to do.

We were created to instinctively band together and reach out for the betterment of one another. We each possess a deep desire to help. An innate desire to see good win. It's inside every single one of us. Yes, even *that* person you're thinking about right now. The one who is the epitome of everything you think is wrong with humanity. It's inside them too.

I know this can seem like a fantasy. That everyone has something in them willing to risk in order to rescue. To join people who don't look like them, talk like them, vote like them, think like them, or worship like them in order to help others who are in need.

That seems preposterous, right? Especially after 2020. That was a year in which a perfect storm of politics, a pandemic, protests, and more showed us the ugly side of humanity. But I want to tell you something true: Every single human being has this desire to help.

Unfortunately, here's what we come up against. This is the

pain point. The rub. The overwhelming amount of news and content and social media chatter that floods our eyes and devices every single day tells us the opposite thing. That the world has gone to hell. That there is no hope for humanity. That our divided opinions have led us to oppression. That the country is just going to get worse from here. That there is no hope for decency in our world. That the whole thing is "us versus them."

All that messaging leaves us in a scary place, where we are merely surviving instead of thriving. But what if I told you that it doesn't have to be this way? Or even better, what if I told you that the world is *not* this way? That's right. What if I told you that the world is filled with compassionate, giving, kind, and loving individuals who do want to help those around them? Full of people like you and like me, many of whom simply need a recalibration to live with the kind of generosity and goodness they were made for.

And I'm not just talking about recalibrating your co-worker who has a bumper sticker that makes your blood boil.

I'm not just talking about recalibrating your aunt on Facebook whose posts are filled with the epitome of everything that is wrong with humanity (or so you think).

No, I'm talking about *you.*

That's right. Because change starts with you.

• • •

Humanity doesn't need a rebuild; it simply needs a recalibration. A reset, if you will. I have come to the understanding that we have all been created in the image of God. I know that's not the belief system you may have grown up in, but it's the crux from which I am writing. It is the basis I am funneling all these thoughts through. Genesis 1 tells us that we were made in the image and likeness of God, and that's an incredible place to start from. Later in the book, we will dive deeper into what "creation" should desire to become. For now, just know that this is my starting place.

To rebuild what we were designed to be isn't our job. That would be an impossibility for us. That falls in someone else's hands alone. We will get to Him later, but for the time being, just go with me toward this recalibration. Toward this reset.

You likely understand the next three words and the power they had—and can still have—over our lives.

Control. Alt. Delete.

These words were our literal rescue. You see, before there were MacBook Pros that simply worked every single time you turned them on, we had these computers called PCs. Now, I know you might still use one and I've heard that they have gotten better, but let me tell you that in the nineties, these things would fill with so much spyware and viruses that even moving the mouse across the screen would become a cumbersome task. So whenever our computers would slow down because of all the stress that was being put on them from all the processes they were having to do behind the scenes, we would simply press those three buttons at the same time.

Control. Alt. Delete.

What would that do?

Well, to be honest, I don't know what happened on the inside of the computer, but I do know that when it would turn back on, things would run much better. It was like a recalibration and reset. I didn't rebuild the entire computer. I didn't add RAM or put a new motherboard in. I simply reset and recalibrated it to its original design.

We can do this.

And who can help the people around you with that recalibration?

It's not gonna be me.

It's gonna be you.

You see, I have seen it firsthand. I have seen this recalibration with my own eyes.

People from both sides of the aisle, people from various faith backgrounds, people who vehemently disagree on politics, policies, protests, pandemics, and deities all coming together for the good of a single human. Putting their opinions and stances and beliefs aside to step up and rescue someone. And I'm not talking about seeing this kind of helping happen in 1985. I'm talking about seeing this happen in 2020 and 2021 and 2022 and on.

You see, deep down inside each one of us (yes, even *them*) is an inherent desire for good. It's not even a desire; it's an actual human reflex inside each of us. This isn't complicated, my friend. We just need to unearth that buried reflex and bring it to the surface of who we are today. And we may have to dig it out of ourselves. Will it take some work? Absolutely. Will it be fun? Absolutely not.

As Curtis walked me back to the barbershop that day in 1985, smelling like the cologne he poured liberally onto his torso, mixed with incredibly strong body odor brought on by his spontaneous workout to chase down a kidnapper, he wasn't thinking about how hard he'd had to work to catch the guy. Curtis wasn't thinking about how much fun he did *not* have sprinting his 250-pound body past Arby's and Sears to jump on top of the kidnapper. No. Curtis was as high as a kite on what he and those other strangers did to help that poor mother and child. They came together to help someone else. They came together. Why? Because that's how we human.

So, are you ready to dig? I've got all the tools you're gonna need. Let's remind the world exactly how to do this.

How to help.

How to hope.

How to human.

SECTION 1

be

1
· · ·

be human

I f you say the year 2020 out loud these days, you will likely get a visceral reaction from most people who lived through that year. Try it. Walk up to someone in your house or apartment or neighborhood* and say, "Look me in the eyes. I want you to say the first word that comes to mind when I say what I'm going to say. Okay? Ready?"

Take a moment and then say, "2020."

I promise you there will be a reaction of some kind. I'm not sure there's ever been a number that elicits such a unified response of disgust. I just tried it with my kids. Ready to hear their one-word responses?

My oldest daughter replied, "Ugh." Not the most poetic answer, but I didn't raise poets. It's okay. My middle child responded with the word *sucked*. Okay. I started to see a trend. My third and youngest kid said, well . . . I can't repeat what he said in this book. He got in a bit of trouble for saying that word.

"What about the year 2019? Or 2018?" I asked. And I went

---

* Or *van*—I see you, #vanlifers!

back even a few more years. My little focus group, which consists of my kids, offered quite a few words, all of which were a lot better than *ugh, sucked,* and %@$#*.

All the words they shared for earlier years consisted of other people's names, or words associated with family trips that they remember fondly. It was astonishing. Nothing but pleasant thoughts for all the other years. Now, I'm not saying that every year prior to 2020 was wonderful for all of us. But I am saying that, by comparison, 2020 was horrible for many of us. Maybe most of us. And to be honest, I don't think it was the pandemic that left the most lasting marks on each person. I think our deeply inhuman response to everything that happened in 2020 left the deepest mark and, for some, the deepest wounds. The year 2020 jacked up humanity. It threw many of us off course, and the problem is that we can't seem to rebound. I mean, I'm writing this book more than two years after the start of the pandemic, and it *still* feels like most of us got knocked off course and can't find our way back. I'm still processing. Still working to understand. Maybe you are too? Why? Because 2020 was about *so much more* than 2020.

• • •

My dad used to tell me an analogy about a ship. If you draw a straight line from the tip of a ship and it continues—going straight—for one thousand miles, it will end up in the place to which it is pointing. But if that boat moves by only *one tiny degree,* for a few days of travel it may seem like that the ship is still heading to the original target. However, that one degree of change will eventually mean that the ship misses the original destination by more than sixteen miles on a 960-mile journey. That simple one-degree adjustment doesn't seem like a big deal, day after day, but as those days slowly add up over weeks, you will arrive at a completely different destination than you originally planned.

So, my question is a simple one: How does humanity get back on course to being the kind of people who run together to help a stranger in need? How do we reset our paths and find our way again after getting knocked from our original course?

It starts with us. We each need to get back—individually—to who we were created to be. We need to return to the original design for who God made us to become. When that happens, something comes alive in each of us. Something wakes up. Something that can join with the people around us to do incredible, brave, exciting, kind, and generous things. The kind of things that a world in pain and uncertainty needs.

God created us to come alive in our original plan and design. The spice of the Italian auntie. The peace of the Kenyan hunter. The sweetness of the southern grandma. We *all* have God's creativity deep inside us, and I believe that the first step in learning how to human is to simply . . .

Be human.

Become who you were created to be. And who were you created to be? The answer, my friend, is, unfortunately, often buried deep within. Buried beneath years and years of trauma, trials, and triggers. Buried somewhere beneath years of slowly growing opinions on issues that may or may not affect you. Buried underneath years of being surrounded by people who look like you, think like you, talk like you, and vote like you. Buried underneath years of watching your favorite television news anchor. Buried underneath years of trying your very best to be human.

Now, I'm not saying anything about whether your years of being buried were good or bad. They could very well have been some of the best years of your life. But the true you—the one I want us to get to and unlock—was around long before the world around you had any influence over your opinion of policies, people, and politics. That version of you existed long before that scary or traumatic thing that happened to you happened. That original version of you is what we are trying to recover and bring back to the surface. And that version of you is the first step in remembering how to human.

Maybe you're asking yourself, *Why is this so important?* Well, it's important because I think that the world has a way of knocking us off course. Somehow we get convinced that we need to change, pretend, or become somebody other than our original selves, even if the alteration is subtle and small and changes us by only one degree. I've seen it firsthand, as I personally watched 2020 do this to so many people. I saw it happen to *me* in 2020 too!

You see, at the core of each one of us, compassion *can* outweigh personal opinion. It's an internal, innate piece of who we are as humans. It's just like the reflex we saw in all those men chasing down the kidnapper in the mall in the introduction of this book. Their compassion outweighed their opinions.

Let me offer you another good example of this in practice. In late 2019, my oldest daughter, Sohaila, became ill. Her illness progressed and got worse over the course of a few days, so much so that we ended up rushing her to Vanderbilt Children's Hospital in Nashville, where they found a mass in her chest and diagnosed her with lymphoma.

I could spend an entire book writing about those twenty-one days. They were filled with miracle after miracle. But what I remember most about those days is the army of people who showed up for us—not just in person but online (especially on

Instagram)—to pray. To lift our family in prayer. To intercede on behalf of my precious daughter.

Prayers were sent up, and I can tell you that healing and miracles were received. When I let everyone on Instagram know that the doctors saw a mass in her chest and were checking us into the oncology floor to begin treatment the next day for lymphoma, I saw thousands of new people show up on my Instagram account to begin to pray. I saw thousands of strangers become family. I saw them storm the gates of heaven on behalf of my baby girl. I saw people I didn't even *know* pray for miracles for our family. And miracles happened. After a day of so many people praying, doctors discovered that the mass had air inside it. A team of doctors came in to tell us that they had never seen a cancerous mass with air in it. So right then and there, they changed the diagnosis to an infection. *Miracle.*

On the flip side, I saw people pray for other miracles that did *not* occur. Like when everyone prayed for her pain to dissipate. Instead, her pain increased. I don't know how to make sense of all that. But I do know that people still showed up every day to keep on praying. And isn't that a kind of miracle? To be so kind and caring to a total stranger? They fell in love with my family, and we fell in love with them. They went to battle alongside us, and I'm forever grateful. You know those friendships that are forged in a fire? This was one of those moments.

Now, imagine with me for a second when in March 2020, just a few short months later, I shared my heart on Instagram relating to the racial injustices happening in America. And imagine my surprise when many of those same people who had gone into battle with me on behalf of my daughter Sohaila suddenly sent me messages telling me how horrible I was and how they wished they had never prayed for us. All because I had shared my perspective on an issue that was incredibly close to me. Imagine my heartache when I got messages from people telling me that they felt they had wasted their prayers.

My heart was crushed. How in the world could so many of these precious people suddenly forget? Forget how to be truly human in the way they were created to be human? How could they show such kindness, generosity, and compassion and then turn around and undo all of it with words of incredible smallness and spite? Even if we disagreed and had differing opinions on matters important to us, did it have to be like *this*? How could they forget so easily?

The truth is that they didn't (forget, I mean). You see, I believed the same things in late 2019 that I believed in March 2020. Perhaps people weren't aware or didn't care enough to know those things about me, or maybe when my daughter got sick, their compassion outweighed their convictions when we asked for prayer for our family.

But the collective stress of the Covid-19 pandemic mixed with racial unrest across the country, tied up with a divisive presidential election, all came together and created a perfect storm. This storm blew many of us off course—even if by one degree, it was enough. And small comments or events that seemed like no big deal the year before suddenly turned into a *massive* deal after a couple months of isolation, lockdown, political jockeying, worry, and stress, and somehow it felt like we ended up landing in an entirely new reality.

. . .

In these times, with many of us overcome by fear, trauma, stress, and division, I think some of us simply forgot who we are. We forgot how to *be*. And that's what we are going to focus on in the first few chapters of this book. How can we find our-selves again? How can we rediscover our inner compass again and get our bearings? Because before we can help others, we must first be willing to help ourselves. And we can't help our-selves unless we are willing to do the hard work to remember who we are in the first place.

Now, I'm not talking about some self-help, live-your-best-truth mantra here. Maybe there's a place for that, but not here. We aren't going to self-help our way back to restoring our faith in humanity again. We only need to recognize who we are so that we can turn around and serve other people. Not so that we are finally free all alone. No. What good is it to find freedom if everyone else around us is in chains? We were created to love and be loved. So, this first step—be human—is only the begin-ning.

Let's look at someone who reflected this idea more per-fectly than we could ever do ourselves. Let's look at the impos-sible example. Let's look at someone who knew who He truly was: Jesus.

Now, listen. I make no apologies that I'm an unashamed follower of Jesus. That I believe He is the literal Son of God. But here's the incredible thing: Even if you don't believe in Jesus the way I do, even if you just think of Him as a historical figure who "did good" in the world, there's no greater example left to us in literature or folklore on how to human.

You can take the supernatural away from Jesus . . .

He still wins the human award.

You can take the whole God thing away . . .

He still wins the human award.

You don't have to believe what I believe about Jesus Christ (you can read all my other books to find out more on that) to come to a consensus that there isn't a greater example of real humanity than Him. I'm not talking about that pastor on TV. And I'm not talking about your fifth-grade Catholic school teacher. I'm not talking about people who may have misrepresented Jesus in your life. *Nah.* I don't have time to write the encyclopedia-length books it would require to undo all that trauma. *Nope.* I'm simply talking about the person of Jesus here. And if you let me, I'd love to allow His life to guide us back to the path we were originally intended to be on. For some, that's a simple one-degree shift. For others, that may be two or three degrees—or more. But what I'm certain of is that it's not much more of a major change than that. You are close. *We* are close.

How do I know this? I know because *He* is close.

2

. . .

be you

"Carlitos, look at me," said my dad, Fermín Whittaker, in Atlanta, Georgia, when I was about five years old. "You are Mexican, okay? You are *Mexican*. Not Black."

My father didn't say these words to me often. But he said this to me enough times during my childhood that I can still see his eyes leaning forward to connect with mine as he spoke, and I remember seeing his face filled with concern and compassion as he did. I didn't know then why he would tell me these things.

However, I do get this weird feeling when I remember those times, almost like he didn't like Black people. But that was kind of weird, because he sort of looked like a Black person. And, obviously, he told me this because I looked like one too. Only just not as much as he did, which is because of my mom. You see, my mom is Mexican. But even she didn't look like the Mexicans I thought of in my head when I heard that word. See, my mom is White. Like as White as Barbara Bush. And there we were in the Deep South, having just moved all the way across the country from Los Angeles, California, to this all-White neighborhood in Atlanta.

My parents spoke Spanish, and I spoke Spanglish. I was just a little kid with a White mom and a Black dad, both of whom spoke Spanish as their first language, and all I wanted to do was make some friends in our new city. But my dad was adamant: I wasn't Black; I was Hispanic. And so that's who Little Los became. I was Mexican/Panamanian/non-Black/ Latino Carlos Whittaker. After these early discussions, I never questioned my dad's reasoning for telling me this again and again, especially every time I would attend a new school. I never questioned him telling me this every time we moved to a new neighborhood. I thought he was simply giving me a history lesson about our heritage. About who I was.

And then one day in second grade, I found out why he was so adamant about this fact.

"I pick the n*!##^. He can probably run the fastest," said the boy when he picked me for his kickball team.

"Um. Hey. Hey, man," I said. "I'm not Black. I'm Mexican."

There was a chorus of laughter. "You are not Mexican, man. Look at you. Look at your *hair*."

He was right. As you know already, I had an Afro that would've made Gary Coleman proud. It was the first time I began to think about the whole thing myself: *Wait a second. Mexicans don't have Afros, do they? This guy is right.* But as I always did, I played into the joke so that the discussion would be over sooner rather than later.

Around the same time, we attended a primarily White church, a wonderful place where I formed many lifelong friendships I still have to this day. It was an extremely beautiful group of humans, and I'm grateful for all of them. All of them except for Scottie.

Every week at our youth-choir practice, Scottie would find me, grab me, hold me with one arm, and smash his large hand into and through my hair, all while yelling to everyone else, "Look, guys! My handprint will stay in Carlos's hair!"

A few of Scottie's friends would gather around and laugh. I remember thinking that all I could do to make this situation go away was to laugh with them. So every week I'd walk into choir practice and try to avoid Scottie until he'd eventually find me and do his trick with my hair for the entertainment of all his friends.

• • •

I never told my parents about those weekly moments with Scottie. And I never told the choir director. I didn't want to make it any worse. I wanted to avoid it all. To keep my head down, as it were.

But every week it was the same. Scottie placed his handprint in my hair. Every week I felt a little less human and a little more like someone else's prop or punch line. Once, I asked Scottie to do his trick to someone else. He replied, "It's not as fun with anyone else's hair."

Scottie graduated when I was a freshman. I felt relief when he was gone. His racist action physically affected me for only about thirty seconds each week, but it terrorized my mind for days leading up to seeing him again.

Now, let's address what you may be thinking. "Carlos, he was just a bully. He was just being mean, and that meanness doesn't make him a racist. Maybe he was just mean and not racist." And to this thought, I would like to say I understand. I do. Why do we have to make *everything* racist? And I'm not trying to do that, I promise. But for the sake of definition for the rest of this book, let's put some handles on my experience. I like to use the definition provided by the National Museum of African American History and Culture when defining a racist idea or action. It "refers to the beliefs, attitudes, and actions of individuals that support or perpetuate racism [the idea that one group is inherently superior to another] in conscious and unconscious ways."

I don't think Scottie was thinking, *I don't like Carlos because he is Black, so I'm going to be mean to him,* but I do think his weekly action of making fun of my hair because it was an Afro was a racist action. This isn't a book on racism, but since Scottie's hair trick is a large part of my story, I feel it's important for you to understand that a racist action doesn't have to be on purpose. People are accidentally racist all the time! Unfortunately for me, Scottie, in his meanness, affected my young Black heart more than if he were just picking on me because I was too skinny. Make sense?

I can't count the number of times I've laughed along to avoid any acceleration of racist actions toward me. I can't count the number of times I've hidden my true emotions and feelings to avoid any acceleration of racist actions toward me. I can't count the number of times I've tried to erase any "Blackness" in me to avoid any acceleration of racist actions toward me.

It was around this season in my life when the Scottie handprint trick started that I began looking a little more into my dad's history. "Dad, where were your parents from?" I asked. "Grandma and Grandpa? Were they from Panama too?"

"No, *mijo,*" he responded. "Grandma and Grandpa were from Providencia. It's a Caribbean island off the coast of Colombia."

There was no internet back then (it makes me feel old to type that), so I ran out the front door and hopped on my Huffy bike. "Thanks, Dad!" I yelled as I took off toward Rehoboth Elementary School. I'd just gotten my first clue (well, besides having a Black dad), and I'd just finished the latest Encyclopedia Brown book about the young detective, so I knew I was going to crack this case. I just needed some help.

Why was it so important for young Carlos to find out who I really was? Well, to put it simply, I wanted to find out so I would know who I was when I was forty-four. You see, knowing *who we are*, knowing *where we came from*, and knowing *why we are*—these are each vital pieces that we need in order to right this ship we call humanity.

• • •

Many people argue that it's not important to know where we came from, because it's much more important to know where we are going. And I understand that idea, at least to a degree. But I will argue that even Jesus Himself knew where He came from and was proud of it. We see that He was unapologetically Jewish. Like He was 100 percent a Jew. He was born of a Jewish mother in Galilee, in the heart of the countryside of Israel. His homeboys, his teachers, his family, and his first followers were all Jews. Jesus worshipped in synagogues on the regular. He preached from Jewish texts. He celebrated Jewish holidays and went on Jewish pilgrimages.

As Shaye J. D. Cohen, professor of Judaic studies at Harvard, once observed for PBS's *Frontline* show, "The gospels have no sense yet that Jesus was anything other than a Jew. The gospels don't even have a sense that he came to found a new religion."* This is so important to remember. Jesus's identity mattered. He worked through it. It was part of Him.

---

* Shaye J. D. Cohen, "Jesus' Many Faces: He Was Born, Lived, and Died as a Jew," *Frontline*, PBS, www.pbs.org/wgbh/pages/frontline/shows/religion /jesus/bornliveddied.html.

At the beginning of this journey together, it's important for us to see how deeply Jesus's identity as a Jewish man affected everything He did. This isn't a bad thing at all. I think we often lose sight of this fact in modern discussions of who Jesus was. We have all these teachers and preachers and sermons telling us that our identity must rest in Christ alone, which sometimes gets twisted into shaming people for celebrating where they come from or their ethnicity or race. I believe the opposite is true: We must know where we came from and who we are to know where we're going. It's okay to be proud of where you're from. It's okay to celebrate the traditions you inherited from your family and the heritage of your ancestors. It's okay because they're what made you who you are. And what made you, most of the time, can guide you into the future.

Let's think for a moment: What is it about yourself, about who you actually are as a human, that you are not likely to put on blast? That you don't want anyone to know? Not because it will hold you back but maybe because you think someone will think less of you? I'm sometimes reminded how back in 2000, my friend Jack, a Muslim from Iraq, did all he could to *not* be Muslim. Just like my dad had me not be Black. But how about you? I think it is important for all of us to find that piece of who we are—the one we might want to hide—and make sure we lay claim to it. Jesus was a Jew. I am a Black Panamexican. What about you? Are you a Scottish immigrant who lives in Ohio and grew up addicted to Ohio State football? If so, *own it.* Be all of it. Don't be ashamed of it. Are you a Mexican immigrant who happens to lean to the opposite political party than most people who look like you lean? Then I challenge you to *lean all the way into that.*

This is really important in being human. Of course there

are things that we are ashamed of. Of course there are things that we don't want everyone to know. But I promise you that if you stop being ashamed of who you are and instead embrace the good, bad, and ugly, you will be a far more confident human. And that's where this thing is headed: toward humans who can be so bold and confident in themselves that they don't even blink when it's time to be bold and confident for others.

How? How do you get there? How do you be human? How do you *be* who you were created to be? It's not just your ethnicity; it's everything about you. There are things about you that you didn't even know *were you*. And those may be just the things that unlock ways to be human. We will get back to that in a few pages, but for now, back to me riding my bike to school.

I parked my bike next to the gym and ran inside, but instead of heading to homeroom, I went to the library. Making my way through the stacks (I can still smell the unique aroma of the books), I beelined for the encyclopedias.* I can't remember exactly how long it took me or how you even look things up in encyclopedias, but I do remember as clear as day landing on the page with facts all about the Isla de Providencia. There was even a tiny black-and-white photo to go with it. The island was an eight-square-mile island off Colombia's northern coast. Spanish is one of the native languages of Providencia, but English and Creole English are also spoken there.

And then I looked closer at the picture. It featured a group of men with their arms wrapped around each other's necks, under a palm tree. They looked a lot like my grandpa. And they

---

* If you have no idea what I'm talking about, think Wikipedia but printed. Yes, on *paper*. (Also, usually the content was based on facts!)

also looked a lot like my friend Boris, who is Black. So I thought, *If they are Black and my grandpa is Black, then why am I . . . not Black?*

I closed the encyclopedia and walked back to my classroom, where it was very obvious that I was the only kid in there who was Black. Maybe my dad knew something I didn't, or perhaps he was keeping something important from me.

When I got home that day, I went to him. "Daddy?" I said. "I looked up where Grandma and Grandpa were from today in the library at school. Are they Black?"

"You are not Black, Carlos," he replied. "Trust me, son, okay?" And it wasn't just what he said that made me wonder what was off; it was how he said it. He responded with a little more fire in him than I was used to seeing, well, *ever*. You see, my dad is a soft-spoken man. He *never* raised his voice. Never *once* made me feel threatened in any way. However, when he responded this time, I felt something from inside him. Somehow he meant this more than he meant most things. And I also felt a little bit like I got in trouble for even asking or for looking up the island in the encyclopedia. There was something there we did not talk about.

"Okay, Dad. I'm sorry."

But that wasn't the last time I went digging for answers about why he didn't want me to be a Black kid in Atlanta. Even typing that sentence out right now makes my eyes well up with tears. *Because now I know why.*

But we'll get to that.

• • •

Is there something about *your* story that you avoid sharing with others in hopes that life will be easier without that part of your story being true? If so, it's all right. You don't have to share every facet of who you are with the world for you to be human. But I will also say that it's vital for *you* to at least know your story inside and out. Both the beautiful parts and the ugly parts of your story are relevant. I have friends who love their southern roots, but they also acknowledge that they don't necessarily love all that comes with those roots. That doesn't mean they don't celebrate the parts they do like or ignore the parts they are embarrassed about; it just means that they *understand*. They see the entirety of who they are and where they come from in order to live in the healthiest way possible.

After that conversation with my dad, for a long time I stopped asking about my background and where I came from. I stopped digging. I stopped remotely looking for the Black side of my story. Until 2019.* I had been not-Black Carlos for years, and then in 2019, my wife, Heather, thought it would be fun for us to do an Ancestry.com DNA test.

I don't even know what I expected. I don't think I realized how I'd brainwashed the Black right out of my story and soul. But when I received my results, they said my DNA was 72 percent Nigerian.

Yes, 72 percent.

Nigerian.

The results stopped me in my tracks. "Did I read that right?" I asked out loud. "Wait, *what*?"

"What does it say?" my wife asked.

"It's says I'm Black," I responded.

"Of course it does!" She was dying laughing. "Your dad is Black. But where in Africa are you from?" She asked so nonchalantly, like she just knew I was African. And of course she

---

* Yeah, *2019*. That's not a typo.

did. My wife has been to all my gumbo-eating Black family Christmas dinners for twenty years!

And that was the moment I realized just how much I had suppressed the Black side of me for my entire life. I had to call my dad.

"Dad," I said when I got him on the phone. "I'm Black. Like *Nigeria* Black."

He laughed.

"Why did you always tell me I wasn't while I was growing up?" I asked him.

"Carlitos, I'm sorry I was so adamant about that," he began. "But when we moved to Atlanta in the eighties, I knew it was going to be much easier for you to be Mexican than it was for you to be Black. If I had to do it over again, I wouldn't do that. But it was all I knew how to do to protect you from the racism that I know you still experienced."

I couldn't say anything. I couldn't even be mad. I understood. Although I was almost embarrassed that I'd refused to even investigate the Black side of my identity and heritage for decades.

"So, can I be Black now?" I asked him, only half joking and half still looking for his approval and permission.

"Yes, son," he replied matter-of-factly. "You can be Black. Because you *are* Black."

This was in 2019. A few months before the year 2020. And little did I know then how much the Black part of me was about to come alive.

Listen, we all have parts of us that need to come alive. You have parts of you that have been hidden and shamed for far too long. And the first step in being human is to step into the fullness of who you are. This is what I was talking about a few pages back when I said that maybe there are things inside you that are you that you didn't even know were there. Things that you can actually stand up proudly and display for the world.

One of the things I ask myself all the time is, "Carlos, what is the last thing that made you jump for joy?" No, seriously. That's what I ask. And when you think about it, it was probably when you were a kid. Like when you got a present for Christmas that you weren't expecting. The rise of emotion would sometimes actually make you lift your entire self off planet Earth. The exuberance that exploded out of your heart and into your legs would cause them to bend and then lift, propelling you into space. And if only for a second, you were suspended in the air all because you received something that made you literally jump for joy. I think those are the things you need to ponder in order to get to the core of who you are. No matter how old you are, you still have excavating and uncovering to do.

How can you do that? Well for starters, I think you need to list those things that make you jump for joy. And if there isn't anything that you can write down, guess what? That is fantastic news. All that means is that you have yet to discover everything that makes you, *you*! How amazing is *that*? Like you have lived your entire life and not even stepped into everything you were created to be! It excites me that there could be thousands of people who suddenly begin to come alive in ways they didn't even know was possible. For some of you it could be taking that DNA test! (Not the Maury Povich talk-show versions, but the kind that maybe wake you up to a part of you that you didn't know existed.)

What are the parts of you that need to come alive?

3

• • •

be love

The year 2020 really started (for most of us, at least) in March. This isn't to say that January and February were a piece of cake or without plenty of news stories to obsess over. I mean, do you remember the massive Australian wildfires that consumed so much of that continent in early 2020? The Australian wildfires would have been the biggest news story of the year in other years. *Three billion* animals died, and the fires burned nearly forty-six *million* acres. The World Wildlife Fund CEO said it was the worst wildfire in modern history. I was gripped and on Twitter praying for God to somehow make it rain where it had not rained in a long time. The images were insane. I have many friends from Australia, and just seeing the looks on their faces let me know how destructive the fire became. "It's like if *all* of America's national parks burned," one friend told me. And that's all it took for me to realize the true devastation of those fires.

But even a short time later that same year, most people barely remembered that story. Why? *Because of Covid, Carlos.* I call it the "Covid Coma." Many of us don't remember anything from the three months prior to widespread lockdowns that began in March. But do you remember the beginning of the pandemic? Of course you do. We all do. We will never forget. It kind of came out of nowhere while simultaneously feeling like a slow-motion avalanche.

• • •

In January 2020, someone from China who follows me on Instagram messaged me. She asked for prayers for her family who lived in Wuhan. She said that there was a virus hitting that community hard. I'm fairly certain I sent her a few prayer-hand emojis and called it a day. And to be honest, it had felt like I prayed for her, because I responded. But had I actually *prayed*? No.

But then as the weeks progressed, I kept thinking back to that message. She was right and knew something I didn't, but since it wasn't currently affecting me, I didn't offer her a human response. And there is something haunting about that memory, because as the weeks moved into March, I along with all of you began to collectively feel the seriousness of the situation without knowing the seriousness of the situation because *we were all pandemic rookies.* Can I get a witness?

It's like we all had a lump in our throats that week before everything locked down. Everything moved in slow motion. At the grocery store, many of us stood in long lines buying food, toilet paper, and paper towels. (Can someone tell me *why* again?) I distinctly remember seeing a scared look in everyone's eyes. We all wore that look. It's the look you have on your face right after a cop pulls up behind you on the freeway, turns on their lights, and speeds past you. That look.

But if you remember, there was also something strangely unifying about the entire Covid-lockdown moment. (At least at the beginning!) Seriously. Do you remember? At least in my circles, it felt like we were united in ways we hadn't been since the terrorist attacks of September 11, 2001. Of course, 9/11 was a devastating, tragic day in America, but somehow it also became a unifying day for Americans, for weeks and even months after. We came together.

I remember when we marked the twentieth anniversary of 9/11. It got me feeling all the feelings. You may or may not be old enough to remember the day well or even at all. This is what I wrote on Instagram on the anniversary:

Before our reaction to tragedy was hammering our thesis through our thumbs upon the six inches of LCD in our hands . . .

Before our reaction was preparing our essays as to who to blame for the world to see . . .

Before our reaction was getting our talking points from our favorite political pundit . . .

Before our reaction was to question those who mourn . . .

Before these phones made us a little less human . . .

Our human reaction was to sprint into the dust . . .

Our human reaction was to link arms together . . .

Our human reaction was to check on our neighbor . . .

Our human reaction was to mourn with those who mourn . . .

We had a human reflex of unity . . .

It's an actual reflex inside us all . . .

And it's still there . . .

I promise . . .

We just have to dig a little.

You see these phones aren't the problem . . .

Our opinions aren't the problem . . .

There were plenty of opinions in 2001 . . .

It's simply that those two mixed together in moments of crisis have made us a lot less human . . .

So as we look back at 9/11 . . .

As we remember and mourn the loss . . .

Maybe remember what it felt like to have a reflex to unite instead of divide . . .

To heal instead of harm . . .

To believe instead of blame . . .

To hope instead of hate . . .

To see instead of slander . . .

It's in us.

We just have to dig a little . . .

The post went viral. Amanda Gorman, the youngest inaugural poet in U.S. history, shared the post on her feed and it took off even more. Then I felt, *What do I do to celebrate when one of the most popular poets of our time decides my words will suffice for her to express her thoughts?*

But other than the honor of Gorman giving my words some small validation, the reason that post resonated with so many people was that it reminded us that we all have a level of compassion built into our DNA as humans. (And yes, in this post, I did blame the evolution of the internet and in some way the advent of social media for staining the fabric of that compassion.)

I saw something uniquely human in the way that we all got back on our feet after that day in 2001, a day filled with so much evil and hate. We got back up. We linked arms with one another, differences aside. There was a sense of unity.

If we look back at the beginning of this whole Covid thing,

if we go back to lockdown, I saw that same sort of sense of unity in America and, at some level, around the world. I know that not everyone was on board with certain policies and procedures and government responses, but I do know that people were much more unified in finding a solution than they would be in just a short matter of time (or, for that matter, are now as I write this).

None of us, except for the *very* oldest, had gone through a global pandemic. This was new for the vast majority of us. Plus, there was fear and uncertainty about what would happen. Those dynamics mixed together and created the (short-lived) sense that whatever happens, we're all in the same boat.

• • •

On the first morning that we locked down, I had an idea. Something I thought would help my neighborhood smile a little bit. I went to the garage and started moving boxes around. It was March, so not too many boxes had begun to pile in front of the recently packed-up Christmas decorations. You know how it goes, right? By the time Christmas rolls back around each year, I'm in desperate need of Marie Kondo to come help me clean out my garage simply so that I can reach my decorations.

I was initially going to pull out the small lawn decoration. The four-foot-tall one. Then I thought, *Nah. They're gonna get the big one.* So, I pulled out the fourteen-foot Santa Claus. I also grabbed a ten-foot piece of plywood, and Heather and I began painting. We painted it white. Then Heather took over with a red can of paint and started painting words on the giant piece of wood.

When she finished painting, I dragged the wood and our

deflated plastic Santa out to the front corner of our yard. We live on a corner of the busiest street in our neighborhood, so I set up the sign and the depleted Santa, aiming them both right at oncoming traffic. After a few pounds of a sledgehammer, I plugged the power cord from the Santa into the extension cord and watched it inflate. In the moment, I felt like Chevy Chase on *Christmas Vacation* staring up proudly at his house full of Christmas lights.

And that's how, within minutes of my impulse decision in the middle of March 2020, we stood a fourteen-foot Santa Claus in our yard who waved at every single car that drove by, with a huge sign next to him that read "Ho Ho Hope. We got this!"

In just a few minutes, we started hearing cars honking as they drove by our house. People began to stop and take pictures of the sign and Santa Claus. I saw kids from the neighborhood walking into my yard with their parents to take photos next to our Covid Santa. This went on for weeks. But there was something special about that first week of Santa. Do you know what it was?

We were all riding through the pandemic together and hoping we'd get through it together. Nobody knocked on my door to ask me if I was going to get a vaccine (if they ever invented one) before feeling a bit of hope from my silly little Covid Santa. Nobody asked me my thoughts on the lockdown or whether we were losing our freedom before honking at the "Ho Ho Hope" sign first. No. It was simple. It wasn't complicated. I find that it rarely is.

Simple. That's the word.

• • •

Let's remind ourselves of the simplicity of things like this. I know that might sound strange coming from a man who is writing an entire book about how we need to course-correct our humanity, but I'm serious. It's *simple*. We only complicate it with our agendas.

As a follower of Jesus, I have spent decades studying His life. I've spent decades trying to be more like Him. And so many times, I overcomplicate being a follower of Him.

Listen, I'm not saying that I don't think it's important to dive into the depths of the Greek texts of the New Testament to better understand who He was. I'm grateful for all the smart people around me who have gone to seminary and the sort to help me have a clearer understanding of Jesus. I'm grateful for my pastors and leaders who study harder than I do and preach incredible messages that inspire and uncomplicate some complicated scriptures. But if we're talking about keeping it simple, that's one thing that Jesus did well. He kept it *simple*.

If you gave someone who had never heard of Jesus one of the gospel accounts of His life—let's say the gospel of Luke—and asked them read it, they wouldn't need a doctorate in order to let you know how Jesus lived and what He was all about. I'm certain after their reading of the gospel of Luke, they would say that Jesus was about two things: loving God and loving people.

See? It's that simple for us.

Love God and love people.

The former accelerates the latter. I don't think that you need to necessarily love God to love people. (I actually know some pretty loving atheists.) But I *do* know that if you fall in love with God, it allows you to love people in impossible ways, because God's love is just that: It's impossible. As in it's actually humanly impossible to love like God did without God Himself injecting into our love. It's also impossibly simple. He loves every single one of us unconditionally. Jesus showed that over and over in Scripture. He simply loved.

Now, some people would try to make you believe that there's some obstacle course you must defeat before you are able to love the world as Jesus did. Some people would like you to believe that it's far more complicated for each of us to love people than it really is. They might try to convince you that love needs some sort of complicated scaffolding for it to truly be love. But I'm here to tell you that's not it. No. It's simple: *Love* them.

And don't go and try to add words like *tough* in front of *love* to make you feel better about certain ways you are humaning. (Yeah, I'm gonna keep making that word a verb, so get used to it, my friend.) Let's stop complicating love. Let's just find people who are hurting and love them.

I didn't go to seminary. I mean, the liberal arts school I attended academically expelled me! Thankfully, we don't need any sort of education to understand how simple loving others and loving God is.

So, go. Grab your blow-up Santa and put it in your front yard in July if it will help someone else feel more loved. Go. Take some cookies to your neighbor for no reason other than knowing that they, like most of us, probably need a reason to smile today. Pay for the person's groceries or Starbucks order behind you. Compliment someone's shoes while taking a walk. What can you do today that will make someone feel loved? It's not going to be as complicated as you think. I promise.

Now, I'm not saying that loving someone can't get complicated. There are certainly situations that we come across in our daily attempts to love others that can easily be defined as complicated, but the beginning of love, the human decision to make someone feel loved—that isn't complicated. Know that we will get into the complexities of love before we're done. But we can't even get to the complexities unless we first take a simple yet profound step.

So let's start here, with the bare simplicity of our humanity. Let's keep *being human* as simple as it gets. Just find ways to love God and love others. I think this simple focus can help heal so many of your relationships.

The thing that may *feel* a little more complicated is loving those people who you absolutely don't feel like loving. Yup. I'm not gonna skip past that. Don't worry—we will talk about this later in the book. But for now, let's just do the simple thing: Go make someone feel loved today. Because I promise you, if you've ever felt that humanity was broken, there's a good chance that a stranger you meet today feels the exact same way. And you can be the reason they may end up cracking a tiny smile on their drive home and think, *Wow, I wish more people did things like that.* They won't even realize that there's a growing army of humans who are doing just that.

Being human.

In Jesus's humanity, He taught others how to love in simple ways. In John 15:12, He stated it so simply: "My command is this: Love each other as I have loved you" (NIV). And then when we take a step back, we see how simply He did this. Throughout His ministry, He showed His love for others by blessing and serving the poor, the sick, and the distressed. I mean, I don't need to do a deep dive into theology for us to understand this part of being human. Copy and paste that lifestyle into our own. We do that. We are love.

· · ·

A while ago, I was traveling in Seattle. I was about to check out of my hotel when I heard a housekeeper singing loudly in

Spanish. Her voice was good. Actually, it was *really* good. I slowly sneaked my way out of my room and toward her cleaning cart in the middle of the hallway. She was still singing. I walked to the doorway, and her back was to me. I didn't want to startle her when she turned around, so I just started clapping slowly. She didn't turn around, and I realized that she had headphones on, so I clapped louder. She must have heard, because she turned around quickly and jumped and gasped while her eyes looked as if they'd doubled in size.

"You have such a beautiful voice. I love it!" I said. But she looked mortified. "Oh my goodness," she said with a strong Hispanic accent. "I'm so sorry, sir. Nobody was supposed to be occupying this floor. I'm so sorry!"

"Please don't apologize," I replied. "I loved it. I have a question. Can I ask you to sing your favorite song and I'll record it for my Instagram audience? Then everyone can love your voice as much as I do." Shocked and a little shy, she agreed. So we did it. She began singing her heart out, watching my phone light up while all these little hearts were flying across the screen. She felt so loved by my crew. "Thank you for that, sir. I've never sung in public before."

"Well, that's just your first concert, I'm sure. Thanks for sharing your gift."

I didn't give her a tip. I didn't make her famous. All I did was tell her that I loved her voice. And in turn, she felt loved. It's that easy.

Because you know what? It's not complicated. The small stuff matters. The little moments when a word or a song can make someone feel seen and bless someone you didn't even know was there. So, what do you say? Love people. Simply love people. Give it a shot.

Watch what happens. *Ho ho hope.*

Now shut this book. Right now. Go find a simple way to love somebody or show them they are worthy of love. I'll help you with that family member you can't stand later. I promise. But first, go find someone you don't know, a total stranger, and love them. It won't increase just *their* faith in humanity; it will increase yours as well.

4

. . .

be compassion

When it comes to compassion, I don't want your *sympathy* as much as I want your *empathy*. But I'm already getting ahead of myself. We'll get to empathy soon enough.

First, let's talk compassion. *Compassion* has been defined as "sympathetic pity and concern for the sufferings or misfortunes of others."* Now, I don't love the first part of that definition (because I think empathy is a bigger deal than sympathy, but there I go again getting ahead of myself). Nah, it's the second half of the definition that, for me, is the sweet sauce of compassion: "Concern for the sufferings or misfortunes of others." That's it. That's the next step. My friend, it's time for us to go to Compassion School.

Perhaps you hear that word *compassion* a lot. It's the third word in a popular church song from the 2000s, Reuben Morgan's "Mighty to Save": "Everyone needs compassion, a love that's never failing."

But hang on. I think I know what you might be thinking:

---

* *The New Oxford American Dictionary*, s.v. "compassion," www.lexico.com /en/definition/compassion.

How in the world can Christians sing that song every single Sunday and walk out those church doors acting the fool? 'Cause I see very little compassion coming out their lives! I know. I get it. I feel and have felt that way often, especially over the past few months and years.

Maybe because it's going to take a little more than a cute melody, some clever lyrics, and some goose bumps to pour true compassion and mercy out on this planet. Maybe it's going to take a realization that we're not going to transform the world by changing opinions but instead by chasing hearts. And how do we chase hearts? *Compassion.* Not just the word, not just a song, but with doing something about the sufferings and misfortunes of others.

In the previous chapter, we were talking about the week lockdown started in March 2020. Seeing a kind of unity among humans was a reaction that seemed to come from all of us. Maybe you recall seeing people playing each other music from their balconies in various cities in Italy, or New Yorkers in lockdown singing to each other from their windows. It lasted only a couple of weeks, but it happened. It was there. *And it is still there.* And to be honest, it's easy to get lazy at doing this human thing when things are going well for us. When things are not in a downward spiral.

It's easy to give money to a person with less when you have money. It's easy to pray for someone who is sick when you are healthy. It is easy to celebrate someone getting pregnant when you have had successful pregnancies. It's just easier to walk the talk of being human when things are going well. But let's think about who is truly being the definition of how to human in all seasons. The people who are not living in the lap of luxury, right? There is something so authentic about their humanity that I think speaks volumes on what they are actually placing their dependence in. Not on if things are going well or not.

Some of the purest humans I have ever come across were in seasons of life that most would call difficult. Why is that? Why would I call their humanity pure? Well, it's because they don't have anything to decorate it with. They don't have a Pinterest life. And whenever you can see humanity that moves you from someone like that, you know that it is pure. I find this every single time I visit a country where the amount of resources they have available is a drop in the bucket compared to what I have here in America. When I go to a village in a country that is poverty stricken and they give me a gift as I walk into their home, I feel the love and humanity from them in ways that I never feel here. I'm not saying that we can't get to the essence of our humanity in more established countries, but I'm simply saying that to truly human, we must be able to do so in all seasons.

At the beginning of the lockdown in March 2020, few of us knew anyone who had gotten Covid. We heard on the news about people getting sick. We heard from a friend of a friend of a friend about people getting sick. But that disease was something that most of us looked at from afar. In some ways, Covid was that distant thing happening in China, something that was only just beginning to scare us here. Do you remember how many of us thought the lockdown was going to last only fourteen days and then it would all go away? Some of us thought that by June, we'd be far past Covid.

Ha! I laugh about this now, because at the time, it made so much sense! We will just lock everything down for a few weeks and stay in our homes and this thing will disappear. (Again, we were all pandemic rookies.) So now I laugh at my lack of pandemic skills. We did all we knew how to do at the time: hope for each other.

Ah, just typing that sentence makes me long for days gone past. Remember those days at the beginning of the pandemic? When we hoped for the best for each other despite what anyone else believed? I want each of us to think about that and make an honest assessment of where we are now. Come on. Right now.

As I write this chapter, I'm still very aware as to how much current culture has affected our ability to show compassion, especially when we see people doing things that we consider impermissible. There are many people who are in need of our compassion right on the other side of our opinions.

. . .

On March 11, 2020, my mom called me from Southern California to let me know that she wasn't feeling well. She and my dad had just gotten home from a wedding in Fresno, and she said she felt like she was running a fever. (Now, this was at the *very* beginning of all the chaos. I honestly didn't even think twice about it being Covid. And now if I so much as sneeze once anywhere, I immediately say out loud, "Not Covid!") The next morning, my mom called me again. Her temperature was now up to 103 degrees. I told her, "Mom, you need to go and get a Covid test. And stay away from Dad."

Now, let me tell you the impossibility here. The first impossibility was that there was no way my mom was going to be able to stay away from my dad. He was in the early stages of dementia at the time and was glued to my mom all day, every day. They lived in a tiny house in Menifee, thousands of miles away from both me and my brother, so my dad couldn't just move in with us. He *relied* on her.

The second impossibility was even finding and getting a Covid test. My mom, with her 103-degree temperature, went from hospital to hospital in Riverside, trying unsuccessfully to get tested. For *an entire week,* she went from hospital to hospital, from clinic to clinic, without being able to get tested. And she was getting worse. Lockdown was only a few days old at this point, and there was no way I could get to her. She Face-Timed me from the emergency room on the night of March 17.

"Mijo, I'm scared," she said. "They are just telling me to go home and take Tylenol, but I feel worse than I ever have."

Here was my sixty-eight-year-old mom, who (spoiler alert) *had Covid* but couldn't get tested or treated. I tried my best not to worry, but the thought of my dad without his primary care-taker—my mom—was almost too much for me to handle.

That was the night I decided to ask the Instafamilia to pray. To pray for her but also to let me know if there was anyone in Southern California that could get her some help. (What's the Instafamilia, you might ask? Don't worry—that's coming.)

And here's the thing: This happened during the season of the pandemic when we hadn't yet lost our collective soul at the same time. It was the season during which people were still *hoping* for each other. Like *hoping* as a verb. Rooting for each other. Rooting for people on the opposite side of the political aisle. Rooting for people who had different religious beliefs. We were all on the same side of this thing and were united in lockdown.

We just wanted to all survive.

When I sounded the alarm about my mom on Instagram, I

saw everybody hope for her. And no one asked if she was vaccinated so that they could decide whether to care. No. People simply *cared*.

Now, let's think about this reality for a second. When someone gets diagnosed with a disease, nobody looks at their history to see if they took care of themselves the way they should have before they choose compassion. Nope. That's not how it's supposed to be done.

We are built as humans with compassion inherent inside us, but much of what we have been through as a society has made us calloused to the point that we've forgotten how and when to use our natural compassion reflex. It's not as if people didn't have strong opinions about things back then; we just didn't let those opinions get in the way of our compassion for others.

People flooded my direct messages (DMs) with offers to help my parents. People brought them dinner. People contacted friends who worked with the Riverside health department. People came through for my mom in all sorts of ways. The biggest thing I remember hearing is that my mom was one of the first "friends" people knew who had Covid. Now, I say "friend" because people on Instagram call me their friend. Like people who have never had a conversation with me but just follow along with my life every day. And so, since I'm their friend, they would say things like "My friend thinks his mom has Covid" to their IRL (in real life) friends. And I would get messages from friends of internet friends telling me what vitamin cocktail to send my mom. And since it was at the beginning, I think there were many people just glued to their phones waiting to see if my mom had Covid.

Compassion was at an all-time high, and it spilled over to my mom's story and the prayers were working. After fourteen days with a solid 103-degree fever, which finally broke, my mom started feeling better. Then by day twenty-one, she *finally* got a test, and by day twenty-five, she *finally* got a result of positive for Covid.

This came weeks after she had already recovered. That's how long it took. Incredible. But I saw my community come together and lift her up because they had compassion for her.

It absolutely baffles me how quickly we forget that this kind of compassion is not only possible but essential. I don't know about you, but I'm ready for us to get back to it. We didn't wait for our vaccinated acquaintances to get hit with side effects. We didn't wait for our unvaccinated friends to get sick enough to go to the hospital. No. This isn't who we are. It's not. I think perhaps we've lost our ability to find the compassion deep within us because it's been buried by more than just our opinions and our politics; it's been buried by our inability to process the avalanche of everyone else's opinions. Again, I want to reiterate that opinions aren't bad. But it seems our constant attempts to fine-tune our own opinions and dull the opinions of others have set us up with impossible expectations. We now have a faulty expectation that compassion should be doled out and limited to only those people who believe the same way we do. Some of us think that people's compassion should somehow be boxed into a political party or persuasion.

But I think that's the opposite of where true compassion lies. I think it's only half-human to find compassion for only those people who think and believe like ourselves. I think true compassion is found *outside* the walls of our various (often arbitrary) bubbles. And the more we try to fine-tune our opinions on issues with podcasts and books and TV shows and conversations that feed our biases, the further away from true compassion we get.

Compassion isn't supposed to be about just those people who stick to your exact belief systems. That's not how Jesus did compassion in His life. When I think about compassion and Jesus, I think about His parable, or story, about the lost sheep:

> The Son of Man has come to save the lost. What do you think? If a man has 100 sheep, and one of them goes astray, won't he leave the 99 on the hillside and go and search for the stray? And if he finds it, I assure you: He rejoices over that sheep more than over the 99 that did not go astray. (Matthew 18:11–13)

Let's think about those ninety-nine sheep for just a second. Like, I'm no sheep, nor will I pretend to play one in these pages, but I do think that the other ninety-nine sheep must have been like, "Hey, Shepherd! Why you leaving us for that straggler? He decided to go on his own and do it his way. It's his own dang fault for getting lost! He had the chance to stick with us, but he decided to risk it." Think of the blame, the resentment, the "He got what was coming to him."

But the Shepherd who had compassion for that one sheep? He left the ninety-nine to go find the one. He left the flock and went after *one sheep.* Where is the sense in that? The sense of love. The sense of compassion. He went to find the one that probably didn't do things the way the rest of those that followed Him did. *He went after the one.*

So here's a good start to getting our compassion back: Go after the one. No, seriously. Go after the one that left and got lost. Who is outside the flock? Who's left out? Who's forgotten, overlooked? *Go after them.*

And don't go after the one simply to bring them back to

wherever you are. 'Cause in these streets, maybe the one left you on purpose. Maybe they left the group you lead because they didn't want to hang out with all the other sheep following you. Whatever their reasons, *go after them*. Go find them wherever they are and let them know that they are loved. Let them know that you care for them. And tell them that you'll love them if they decide to come back and hang with you and that you'll love them just as much if they don't come back at all.

Because the point of going after the one isn't necessarily to bring them back; the point of going after them is to show them true compassion, and that kind of compassion is what has been missing in our world in recent years. If we want to get back to being human, we must recover our compassion.

So, who's it going to be?

Who is the person in your life whom you need to go find to flood them with compassion? The wonderful thing about this little exercise is that it's not even about them receiving the compassion from you; it's about you giving them compassion so that you can be reminded that you have it in you to give.

Are you *ready*? The ninety-nine are out there. *Set?* Good. Now *go*.

5

• • •

be justice

I mentioned earlier that 2020 felt like the perfect storm. It was created by a cocktail of fear and injustice—a pandemic that forced us all to be home and, on our devices, watching each other more intently than we had ever watched each other before. It wasn't *all* bad, though. In between all the new podcasts that were launching and the daily Instagram Live shows that every celeb was putting out there were moments of us thinking, *So, this is what slowing down looks like?*

You remember the day you saw it. I know you do. You saw someone walking past your window whom you had never seen before. Like ever. And then you saw them the next day. At the same time. And then you saw them the next day again. At the same time. These *strangers* were our *neighbors*! That's right. Suddenly our little cul-de-sacs and streets looked like Central Park on a warm spring day. I met more neighbors during lockdown than I had ever met on every street I had ever lived on *combined.**

---

* Now, this could also be a testament to my inability to make friends, but that's for another book.

I live in a neighborhood in South Nashville. It's the cutest little hood. Everyone takes care of their yards and the homes were all built in the 1950s. Suddenly all these kids were out on their bikes all day, every day. Parents were zipping around in their golf carts having drinks in the driveways and sharing their latest and greatest mimosa recipes. We took our family walks around 6 P.M., right before the sun set. We would slowly make our way around the block. Slowly only because Sohaila was still recovering from her twenty-one-day stay at Vanderbilt Children's Hospital. Her lungs were still wounded from her histoplasmosis (that's what it was, by the way—a lung infection), and our walks became victory laps for her. Every day they became a little bit easier. So, when I say it wasn't all bad, that is why. Listen, I love my family, but there has never been a time where we took daily walks together talking about life. It was such a sweet and unexpected gift.

On most of these walks, my son (Losiah) and I would throw or kick some sort of round object. It rotated from tennis ball to football to Frisbee to soccer ball.

"Go long, Lo. I'm going to punt this football as high as I possibly can." So Losiah went long and I tossed the football into the air and gracefully waited for it to begin falling toward my rapidly accelerating right foot. With all the flexibility of a rusted folding chair, my leg sprang forward and connected with the ball. I was *shook* as to how high this ball went.*

"Dad, no!" Losiah screamed. I came out of my daydream of NFL stardom. The ball was unfortunately not going anywhere near him. It was going high, all right, and in a long beautiful

---

* Shook almost to the point of convincing myself during the seven seconds it was in the air that I should try out to be the punter for the Tennessee Titans. I *smoked* that ball!

arc . . . but in the opposite direction. It landed on the roof of a house to my left and bounded down in front of one of the windows. "I got it!" I yelled and immediately started going toward the house. Then I felt Heather's hand grab mine. "Wait, babe," she said. "Why don't you let Losiah go get it?" That was all she said, but of course that was not all she said. Because the look on her face was saying a little bit more.

You see, we pretty much live in an all-White neighborhood. There are a few families of color, but it's not exactly the picture of diversity. What she was *also* saying was that she didn't want her Black husband to be kneeling below a window and surprise the owner as my head popped up after retrieving said ball. And not that the owner of that house was a racist Ku Klux Klan member or anything. Of course not. The likelihood of that was pretty small. But . . . but what? That was the thing. We just can't quite be sure.

See, this is something just a little extra that we must think about on our walks in our neighborhood that most of our neighbors don't have to think about. And I could pretend that this makes me sad, but I'll be honest: This is just a normal thought in my day-to-day. When I move into new neighborhoods, I always make sure to introduce myself to as many neighbors as possible in order for them to know: THERE IS A BLACK MAN THAT WILL BE RUNNING AROUND EXERCISING. Sometimes early in the morning and sometimes later in the evening. I just need them to know I belong.

So Losiah went to retrieve the ball and we went on our way.

Little did I know how much this small moment was about to weigh on my heart. You see, it was a few weeks later that the news of Ahmaud Arbery came out. I remember the specific feeling of my heart leaping into my throat when I saw the video. Two armed White men in a truck chasing after an un-

armed Black man down a backcountry road in southern Georgia. Literal nightmare scenario. (And when I say literal
nightmare, I mean that I have had a nightmare of this exact
thing happening to me. And I promise that many of your Black
friends have had this nightmare as well. Why? Because it's not
a far-fetched idea.)

I think about this all the time. A few weeks back, I stayed at
a super-vibe Airbnb in North Dallas. The neighborhood was
very nice. I had an early-morning call time, so I woke up crazy
early to go run. Like, the sun was about to rise. I put on my running shoes and basketball shorts (I forgot my running shorts),
stretched my incredibly unlimber legs (imagine a giraffe trying
to sit cross-legged—you're welcome), and then put on my
smartwatch to download the latest guided run from the service
I use. As I burst out the front door, suddenly it hit me: *I can't go
run. Not at this hour. Not in this neighborhood.* And as quickly as
I'd charged out that door, I charged back in. I made a decision
that not many of my friends would ever have to make.

• • •

Back to 2020. Now, I need you to remember how a few chapters back, I was just stepping into the Black part of who I am.
To most of my online friends and followers, I was just Carlos,
the author, who would come speak at your church and maybe
make your heart swell with endearing stories about my family.
I was the safe non-White guy that White evangelical churches
could bring in who would not stir the pot. I was the safe non-
White guy who documented the birds in his front yard. Most
of my tens of thousands of Instagram followers were White
conservative Christians.

And I loved them. Why? Because for most of my life, *I was*

them. Except the being White part. I went to their schools. I went to their churches. I was determined for most of my life to be as White as possible. That was until a few chapters ago. So there I sat, staring at my phone, watching my nightmare scenario play out on Twitter. Watching that video of a Black man being hunted. And to make matters worse, I was seeing so many of my White friends *defending the men who shot Ahmaud*. My mind was spinning. If my friends were defending those men, if my friends who loved me and were in my own wedding were on their side, then I could only imagine that those who simply followed me on social media were also feeling that same way. I sat in the discomfort for an entire day before I felt compelled to say something. Then I went downstairs into my basement, turned on the video lights, sat behind my desk, and hit record on a video that would change my life. Only not in the way I had originally intended. Let me explain.

You see, the video that I made was titled "How to Help the Black Community in This Moment . . . If You're Not Black."* It was the most pointed video I had ever made regarding racism in America. But the funny thing is that it's such a kid's book of a video. Like so sweet and simple. As in it's so kind and I call nobody out. But when I made it, I remember feeling like this was the most controversial thing I had ever created. Remember, to the thirty-three thousand or so people who followed me on Instagram, I was the bird guy who loved Jesus; I was definitely not the Black guy who loved justice.

The caption of the video was simple and sweet. I made sure to make the video and caption as inclusive as I could to people

* Carlos Whittaker, Facebook, May 8, 2020, www.facebook.com/Carlos Whittaker/videos/how-to-help-the-black-community-in-this-moment-if -youre-not-black/526104398295352.

across all party lines. It was potent because it was the first time, but it was also soothing and not jarring.

"Don't post it. You will lose so many followers," I kept saying out loud, over and over again. But then I would remember the Ahmaud video. And then I would remember what I was seeing so many friends of mine post on their Facebook pages: reasons why the shooting was justified. Reasons why this death was okay. And the more I thought about them holding their phones in their hands and coming up with the exact words that would give legs to their arguments and then typing them with their thumbs and posting them on Facebook, the more I thought, *How can I not post this video?* And so I did. I posted it (and it automatically fed to Facebook). I posted it at II P.M. Not the most ideal time to post a video on Instagram. But posting that video was as much for me as it was for anyone who would watch it. I felt like I was obedient to the call in my life and who I was, so I went to bed feeling as though a weight had been taken off my shoulders.

That was until I woke up at 8 A.M. and opened Instagram. The comments were mind-blowing. So many people who'd followed me for years were yelling at me (I mean, it felt like they were yelling, because they kept using all caps) to wait for all the information to come in before I rushed to judgment. And then I looked up at my follower count. My heart dropped. I went from thirty-three thousand people following me on Instagram to twenty-seven thousand. I had lost six thousand followers overnight, and the number of those leaving kept growing. They were dropping like flies. By noon, I had lost almost eight thousand followers. *Lord, did I make a mistake? This is the platform that pays my bills, Lord. I can't afford to lose these followers during this pandemic. Oh, dear God, I'm scared I just ruined my career!* These were the prayers that I was lobbing up into the sky. I felt like I had, in a single moment, ruined my career.

So I did what any first-time justice fighter would do: I clicked on the three little dots at the top of the Instagram video that I uploaded, and a drop-down menu appeared. I hovered my finger over "delete video." My heart was pounding. I needed to put a bandage over this gaping wound in my social media before I bled out all my followers and was left with nothing. Two deep breaths and then I did it. I hit "delete video."

As my finger went down toward the screen, I couldn't believe I was giving up. I couldn't believe that this was who I was. I was such a weak people pleaser. Ugh. But alas, I didn't have time for a shame session, as I needed to stop the bleeding. I made the decision. I was deleting the video. Only there was a small problem. After I hit "delete video," another prompt popped up. My screen now said, "Are you sure you want to delete the video?" It hadn't deleted. It was asking me one more time. I wish I could tell you that I had some God moment. I wish I could tell you that I heard clearly from God in this moment. But no. I just clicked cancel and didn't delete the video. I mean, maybe that second prompt *was God*.

And for another second, I was so angry at myself for almost deleting it. And then I got angry at those who were leaving. I got angry because I realized they weren't really following me; they were following a caricature of me. They didn't want to be confronted with the part of me that was coming alive, that was waking up. But then the anger went back to me again. How could I not have created a space that was safe enough to have those sorts of hard conversations? *Lord, You will leave the right people here. You will bring the right people here.*

By midnight, my follower count was twenty-two thousand. I had lost eleven thousand in twenty-four hours. It had taken me more than six years to grow my platform to thirty-three thousand, and in a single day I had wiped out a third of them by standing up for injustice.

I thought, *Well, I guess my account is now about robins and racism,* and I got up to go for a run around my block. Almost as much for Ahmaud as for me.

. . .

It seems like this being human thing is going to cost us something, doesn't it? I mean, if we are truly going to be justice, then we must know that it is going to cost us something. One of the comments that fired me up the most that day was from a commenter who (I paraphrase a little) essentially said, "Stop being so political. Social justice is nowhere in the Bible. Just stick to Scripture and stop making me feel bad for being White. Point people to Jesus, not injustice." This person had been a regular commenter on my account for *years,* and when I clicked on their profile, they had blocked me.

Let's bring this back to the man we are trying to model our human existence after again: Jesus. Not your pastor. Not that Instagram pastor. They are not the goal, remember? We are simply trying to be like Jesus.

And I just want to let anyone wondering know something. Jesus and justice go together like copy and paste. Jesus and justice go together like Jim and Pam. Jesus and justice go together like tacos and Tuesdays. Jesus and justice go together like . . . okay, I'll stop. (But that was fun.)

So (especially if you're doubtful) let's go ahead and spend a minute unpacking the justice side of Jesus's humanity.

You see, I think Christians do a disservice to the gospel when we take the cultural and local context away from the ministry of Jesus. Somebody told me once that He would never say Black lives matter. Jesus would obviously say that all lives matter.

Okay, I get it. Jesus lived on this earth for the purpose of *all lives*. Absolutely. But guess what? When you read the Gospels, you simply cannot come away thinking that Jesus was not very targeted and specific about people groups that were oppressed. I mean, reading the Gospels, you can make a case not only that Jesus would have said Black lives matter but that He also would have said Samaritan lives matter.

Gentile lives matter.

Jewish lives matter.

Leper lives matter.

Why? Because He literally showed us. The first Christians in the Bible were Jewish. They were God's chosen people from back in the Old Testament. And anyone else that was not Jewish in Scripture was labeled as a Gentile. Repeatedly, Jesus showed that both Jews and Gentiles were important, also without even lessening the identity that they had in their respective cultures. And the Jewish religious leaders were not at all happy about Jesus demonstrating that not only Jewish lives mattered but Gentile lives as well. They were so "not happy" that they ultimately put Jesus to death! The following are a few places in Scripture where Jesus was *all about* the people outside the religious spaces where He taught:

- Jesus praised the centurion (Gentile) faith in Matthew 8:10: "I assure you: I have not found anyone in Israel with so great a faith!"
- Jesus praised the Canaanite woman's (Gentile) faith: "Woman, your faith is great. Let it be done for you as you want" (15:28).

- Jesus praised Nineveh, a "Gentile" city: "The men of Nineveh will stand up at the judgment with this generation and condemn it" (12:41).
- Jesus praised the queen of Sheba (a Gentile ruler): "The queen of the south will rise up at the judgment with this generation and condemn it" (verse 42).

Repeatedly, Jesus proved that He was fighting for justice of not only *His* people but *all* people (who ultimately are His people).

Jesus was not vague in His standing up for oppressed people groups, but we try to simplify who He was to make living our Christian lives a little more comfortable. I get it! It's a lot harder to simply have conviction than it is to place action behind our conviction.

Jesus spoke the truth. He shattered the status quo. He spoke up for marginalized people again and again. His agenda was bigger than politics or culture wars. It was *human*. You see, Jesus was and is interested in seeing specific people groups set free. He was completely interested in those forgotten, overlooked, oppressed. We can't escape it, so instead we join it.

This means that to human, you must put action to your conviction. So, what is that going to look like?

Let's look at a clear example in our day and age. Right after Pope Francis became the pope, he invited the leaders from Palestine and Israel for prayer in the Vatican. There was so much drama behind this because he was the first pope to ever put this sort of action behind his conviction.

What that looks like in our lives is to ask who the people are that are outcast by our current segment of society. Whether it be because of political ideals or moral ideals, who are these people? When you begin to get some names or segments, then you simply go to them and find out what they need. And then you give it to them. Remember when I said I didn't want to complicate this more than it needs to be? That's it. Justice is standing up for someone who cannot stand up for themselves, even if you may not agree with everything that they are. One thing that you can connect over is they are human and so are you.

I'll also state that I think to get to the sticking point of this idea of being justice, there is going to have to be some risk involved. Like if it all feels too safe, take up the risk factor a bit. Level up the risk by asking yourself if you will lose any friends by taking a stand. I'm not saying that you must sacrifice friends to be justice, but I am saying that it may happen. And the beautiful thing is that you may lose them for a minute, but the more they look at you and what you are now about, the more they will realize that they actually want to be part of justice as well. The more they will realize that to be human is to be justice.

So many people who left me in 2020 have made their way back to my social channels. And there isn't a giant banner waiting for them that says "I knew you'd come back!" There is simply a smile and a welcome back. Because deep down, everyone believes in justice. And I think if we start by simply letting those in need of our justice know that they matter, that will open us up to relationship that will in turn lead us to being able to advocate for them in better and brighter ways.

You have it in you. You have this justice muscle. And you can literally start using it today.

Who outside your group needs your support? Go fight for them and build bridges that without justice being involved would never have been built.

6

. . .

be wonder

There are two types of people in the world. There are people who believe that birds are real, and people who believe that our feathered friends are not real but rather are robot spies. Sent by the government. To secretly record everything that we are doing. After the government "genocided" *all birds*. Or at least this is what the Birds Aren't Real organization would have us believe.

Or would they? Originally started (according to *The New York Times* as "a parody social movement with a purpose")* to make the point of how easily people can be convinced of nonsense through persuasive disinformation, Birds Aren't Real has held marches and rallies, a protest outside Twitter headquarters, a whole line of merchandise (featuring slogans like "If it flies, it spies!"), billboards in big cities like Los Angeles and Memphis, episodes of *The Truth Report* on YouTube, and (at the time I'm writing this) 406,000 followers on Instagram.

---

* Taylor Lorenz, "Birds Aren't Real, or Are They? Inside a Gen Z Conspiracy Theory," *The New York Times*, December 9, 2021, www.nytimes.com/2021/12/09/technology/birds-arent-real-gen-z-misinformation.html.

(The first post on that account shows a video from October 26, 2001, in which a line of semi-trucks release thousands of "robot birds" into the sky after the government had supposedly eradicated all birds.)

The fact that an outrageous prank like this would not raise that many eyebrows in the competing marketplace of ideas that is the world right now is ridiculous and sort of horrifying. *What is this place?* we might wonder. *What are we all doing?* Something is not okay with us. Something is not okay with our culture.

• • •

One thing many of us learned as the world lockdown went from fourteen days to twenty-one days to four weeks to six weeks is that we had never, ever been forced to slow down like this. Like, ever. We went from a hundred miles per hour to three miles per hour in twenty-four hours. Do you remember? I need you to because those weeks hold something very human for all of us. They hold a key to our humanity that we must hang on to or we may never be able to get it back.

What's that key? The key was the lack of speed.

My generation grew up with Need for Speed movies. I'm going to start a series of movies called Case for Brakes.

How well do you think that will do? LOL.

I mention all the time that the average human being moves at three miles an hour and there is absolutely nothing that we engage in anymore that moves at only that speed. Absolutely nothing. From the way we fall asleep to the way we wake up. From the walk to our cars to the drive to the office. From meeting to meeting, we are moving at a hundred miles per hour, and there is nothing about us that was created to move at that pace. And then suddenly this horrible worldwide crisis forced our hand. It forced us into being a little more human.

How exactly did we begin to be more human in the slower pace of life?

Sourdough.

Yes, that's right.

Before your very eyes, every single person on earth was making sourdough bread. Because what else were they supposed to do while they just sat around at home waiting to see if humanity would survive or not? Well, make bread, of course! Not only sourdough but gardens. Everybody was planting a garden. This pandemic had suddenly forced us to stop moving at the speed of light and start moving at the speed of life.

We rewound about three hundred years in speed. And do you know what began to happen? We began to heal. Now, I'm not going to over-romanticize lockdown. I know that there was so much tragedy involved in what was happening. Death was ravaging our planet. Loneliness was sweeping across the globe. Suicides were spiking. I'm not painting this as a one-size-fits-all moment. But we cannot ignore the truth that we had been barreling along as humans, going faster and faster like an avalanche down the side of a mountain, picking up more and more debris, and we needed to slow down. So much that the world forced us to. And in the long run, I think we will all be better for slowing down.

As I sit here and type, those few weeks and months of being forced to slow down are becoming more and more a distant memory. I'm not seeing near as many people showing off their sourdough-bread cracks as I used to. I'm not seeing near as many people showing off their new plants as I used to. We've picked up the pace again. But if there was ever proof that we had tapped into a long-lost part of our humanity during lockdown, I think it can be found not only by looking at the impact the downtime had on us as humans but also by looking at the world around us and the impact it had on it.

You all saw the tweets and the news stories. You saw the videos.

While we were locked down, the earth was suddenly making a healing sigh. A breath that we didn't know the earth needed. During lockdown, we saw more than 80 percent of the cars that normally are on the roads suddenly disappear, which led to blue skies that most people living in metro centers across the planet had never seen. In Los Angeles, the air quality improved 80 percent. In Kanpur, India, a city with the worst air pollution, there was a video a man took as he climbed onto his roof and started screaming for his family to join him. He was frantically yelling for his father to get up to the roof as fast as he could, for he was seeing something that he had never seen before. This man had lived in this city his entire life, and for the first time ever, he was able to see not only the blue skies, which would have been a miracle in and of itself, but also the Himalayas in the distance. He told a reporter that he did not know the mountains were that close.

We saw videos of dolphins swimming in the canals in Venice, Italy.

We saw sea turtles coming back to beaches that they had not been able to nest at for decades. On the paths near the Golden Gate Bridge, we saw birds nesting that we had not seen nesting in decades. The earth was taking a breath, and we were too.

Let's think about how we have existed from the dawn of humanity until about a hundred years ago. I'm not a history buff, but I'm fascinated by the advancement of technology and the different ages that humanity has gone through, from the Renaissance era to the Industrial Age to this Information Age we are in. Things have sped up so rapidly over the past twenty years that I can't imagine what it's done to the makeup of our souls.

Notice I didn't say our *brains*. I believe that we can and are constantly evolving. There are scientific studies that prove that our brains are evolving, that our bodies are evolving. But you know what I don't think is evolving? Our souls. I believe our souls were created by God in a way that was, is, and is to come. I believe that we were created in His image, and let me tell you something: His image isn't changing, and neither are our souls. So as the world continues to speed up, the question we are left with is this: Are we supposed to just go along for the ride, or are we supposed to take what nature gave us in 2020 and lean into that as much as we can? More and more, we are carrying limitless access to practically infinite media *in our pockets*. We suddenly know more than we ever have. We suddenly have lost all semblance of awe and wonder.

The amount of information accessible to us has absolutely ruined a part of who we were created to be as humans. The fact that we can find out whatever we want whenever we want isn't human. It's not. It's ruining a part of us that I think we didn't know was there to ruin. What if we were created for a much simpler life? What if we were created to not know as much as we know? I'm being serious. For most of humanity, we have known what we needed to know to survive and thrive. Everything was much smaller in scale up until recently. Everything we needed, we got from our local communities. From food to relationships to information, we knew and cared for what was around us. Not until the last 150 years did we even know what was happening as far as a few states away, much less across the globe. We knew what the needs were in our towns and provinces, and we focused on that. We were rightfully enraged by things that happened around us, but because we knew the problems, we were able to fix them. We shopped at our local market. We worshipped at local churches. We read local news. We didn't even have the opportunity to know of most tragedies happening half a planet away—or even a few states away. People were still people, but the flow of information happened at a human pace and a human scale. Now? Well, *now* we can be enraged about everything happening across the globe, and also we are able to know anything in five seconds flat. Our imaginations have become stifled because we don't need to use them anymore. We have become less human even though we have access to more information. Why? Because being human was never about information in the first place.

. . .

Once again, I'm not going to overexaggerate our need to return to a simpler life. I'm so grateful for technology. I'm so grateful for advancement in medicine and the speed in which we can diagnose things. I'm just asking a simple question as opposed to giving a simple answer. The simple question is this: Were we created for this sort of speed, this sort of knowledge?

Note that speed and knowledge aren't inherently bad. They are used for so much good. So we must start to ask, *What* should slow down? *What* should remain unknown? How could slowing down help our mental health? How could not googling everything increase our awe and wonder?

Let's go back to looking at the life of Jesus and the pace at which He lived and His thoughts on wonder.

First, let's just talk about His pace. Jesus had a busy ministry. He was always going from one place to another. But He moved at what I like to call God Speed. And what speed was that? Three miles an hour. That is how fast a human walks.* Unless you are a mall walker or Olympic speed walker. By the way, have you ever tried to speed walk like an Olympian? You will pull a hammy if you aren't careful. It's so hard. You must have loose hips. You must stretch. And you end up looking strange. Why? Because we weren't designed to walk that fast. That's why it looks so strange to see speed walkers at the Olympics. It's not natural.†

As Jesus traveled the Holy Land, dropping miracles, signs, and wonders everywhere He went, he did it at three miles an hour. There is no mention of Him hopping on a chariot to get to Galilee faster. There aren't stories of the twelve disciples hooking their horses up to a tree after they made it to Antioch. Other than that donkey into Jerusalem on Palm Sunday and some boat travel (still at a very human pace!), they walked everywhere. And I can only imagine that pace allowed Jesus to get the most out of His human body while He exerted everything while He changed the world.

I took a trip to the Holy Land a few years back, and while we were driving from town to town that Jesus was walking to, I just kept looking out the window of the road thinking, *Jesus walked these roads!* And I kept reflecting on how much conversation was had with the boys on these walks. Like, we do hear about some of what they were talking about in between all the parables and teaching, but we know we are catching only a fraction of a fraction of these rich convos. Yet I do know they connected with each other in a more natural way than we do

---

* "What Is the Average Walking Speed of an Adult?," Healthline, www.healthline.com/health/exercise-fitness/average-walking-speed.

† Kinda like the people who mix their food up at Thanksgiving. My wife does that. She has her strawberry pretzel salad all mixed in with her green bean casserole and her mashed potatoes and gravy. That is not natural!

today, mostly because of the lack of ability to move fast or connect with people outside His physical locations. It provided such great connection for Him as well as His community. It allowed them to be so *human*. And that God Speed also allowed for wonder. For connection.

Jesus was *all* about the wonder. I mean, He loved teaching in parables—the perfect way to spark wonder in someone's mind. One of my favorite stories of wonder was when Jesus was resurrected from the dead and decided to have some fun with two of His friends.*

So, it was the same day that Mary and Martha had gone to Jesus's tomb with spices they had prepared for His body and they found no body. Where was He? Well, apparently, He was walking down the road to Emmaus, following two of His disciples. Scripture tells us that the disciples were walking along the road discussing everything that had taken place the past few days (which was a lot). Now, I don't know how busy those roads were back then, so I don't know if anyone was around for the next part, but the story continues with Jesus walking up to them and asking what they are talking about. (Remember, this is the risen Jesus pretending to be clueless. I love it.) They stop, look at Him, and, exasperated, answer in the most human way: "Are you the only one who doesn't know what has happened round here the past few days?" That's my paraphrase. Luke 24 says,

> The one named Cleopas answered Him, "Are You the only visitor in Jerusalem who doesn't know the things that happened there in these days?"
> "What things?" He asked them.

---

* Yes, Jesus had fun. Why? Because He was *human*.

What things? I'm shook. Jesus was playing them. Also, take notice. They don't recognize Him. It says that Jesus kept them from recognizing Him. Look at Jesus using His miraculous power to pull a fast one on His friends. I just love the wonder and whimsy of this moment.*

The rest of the story goes on and leads to the disciples discovering who He is, but I want to stop at this principle: Being human means purposely bringing wonder into your God Speed life. That's right. Jesus walking and spreading wonder. I mean, how is that for a recipe? What are some simple ways that you can specifically slow down this week? Maybe take a walk. And no, that doesn't mean a run. That means a walk. Slow down life. Don't take your phone on the walk. Experience things around you that maybe you haven't experienced before because you have only *driven* that road. Another thing I love to do is not use GPS to get places. What happens when you do that? You end up getting lost. I think getting lost is something that we don't do anymore that allows us to tap into our humanity. Here's the thing. Humanity, up until the past hundred years or so, used to get lost all the time. And I think there is something beautiful about it. I think getting lost opens our senses in ways we have long since forgotten.

There is something human about finding our way. We have lost this with Siri, Waze, and Google. We almost need to relearn what it looks like to get lost. One idea is to turn *off* your phone when you are going somewhere. Revert to 1992, when you had to write down directions *before* you left home and then follow those directions to get where you're going. I did this last week and I loved it. I had to stop and ask for directions three

---

* I don't know how Jesus kept them from recognizing Him, but I like to think maybe it was like an *Undercover Boss* moment. A divine disguise!

times. The interaction I had with the gas-station attendants pulled us all back into the seventies. It was incredible! Want to leave your phone on? That's fine. You can still get lost. This is something I love to do. And it increases my wonder in a single moment.

Slow down. Wonder more. You might just find that God Speed feels more human.

· · ·

Back to the birds. For me, it all started in 2019 when I rescued a baby robin out of her nest after a great horned owl murdered her siblings the night before.* Even the most calloused of hearts will be swayed by her comeback story. Anyway, during quarantine I took my love of my backyard birds to a whole other level. Since it was springtime, there were birds building nests *everywhere*. And yes, I placed cameras above all their nesting spots. I had live running commentary on all their nest building and egg laying. The Instafamilia fell in love with all the birds. Robins and cardinals and bluebirds. But I never really told everyone *why* I loved the birds so much. You see, it all started when I had a massive rise in my anxiety. It was too much. The speed of everything seemed to never slow down. Life became suffocating. It was a scary season and a relapse into the anxiety that I thought I had crushed in the past. One morning when I woke up to my heart racing a million miles an hour for no apparent reason whatsoever, I got up and ran outside. *God, make it stop,* I pleaded. I took a couple of deep breaths

* It might just still be in my highlights on my Instagram. Look for "LALA Lives."

and started my daily bargaining with God: *Do things for me and I promise I'll do something for You.*

But I'll never forget how as I began this battle, this robin landed a foot in front of me on the railing. He stood there, quickly snapping his head side to side, looking me up and down. I don't think a wild bird had ever landed that close to me with the sole purpose of judging me. That's what I felt like was happening. After a few seconds of staring at me, he hopped down into the yard, and at the exact spot he landed, he stuck his beak in the grass and pulled out a *humongous* bug. After swallowing it in a single gulp, he looked at me again before jumping to another spot and this time pulled up a mealworm. Gross. He swallowed it whole and hopped to another spot. Every single time he stuck his head into the grass, he would pull out another meal. Then he flew back up into the canopy above me. I stood up and walked out from under my porch and looked up. There were birds everywhere. It was like a suburb of birds up there. My yard probably has a bird homeowner association. There were so many birds up there chirping and hopping down and eating and flying up and chirping. They were having a blast. And then that robin flew back down to the grass and looked at me again. (I'm going to pretend it was the same robin, *'cause of course it was.*) He gave me another robotic look (that was for you robot bird people) and then flew off. It was as if he were telling me, "Hey, man. Look at me. I hop down here whenever I want, and I am taken care of. I'm a freaking bird. And I don't have a worry on planet Earth. Why are you worrying? Don't you think that God cares for you just as much?".

That's what I felt like he was saying. And then I ran to grab my Bible. I remembered that Jesus had said something like what the bird was robotically sending to my brain with its government mind-controlling brain waves.

> I tell you, do not worry about your life, what you will eat or drink; or about your body, what you will wear. Is not life more than food, and the body more than clothes? Look at the birds of the air; they do not sow or reap or store away in barns, and yet your heavenly Father feeds them. Are you not much more valuable than they? Can any one of you by worrying add a single hour to your life? (Matthew 6:25–27, NIV)

Here we have Jesus explaining what I had just seen, and it shook me. I needed to be more like a bird. I needed to look more at birds. They weren't hustling. They did what they were created to do and then sang about it.

They would eat and then sing. They would build a nest and then sing. If a bird life doesn't preach to us, then I don't know what will.

I'm just grateful that we have the opportunity to *not* know things. Yes, knowledge is amazing and very helpful in some situations. And the speed at which we can find things out will save us in certain situations. But how about in all the other situations we decide to slow down and wonder? To be simpler in mind and in spirit?

I think that holds a key for many of us who are trying to be a little more human. So, the task at hand is simple. Slow down. Wonder up. Be more like birds and you'll be more human.

That's a conspiracy I can believe in.

SECTION 2

see

7

. . .

see humans

noticed it by about Gate 67 in the Delta terminal in the Detroit airport. As we approached the gate, the demographics of the people surrounding my little multicultural family began to shift. One by one, the travelers surrounding us went from Black to Asian. From White to Asian. By the time we got to the gate, we were surrounded by 80 percent Asian. That's when I looked down at my son, Losiah. He had a grin on his face that I don't think I had ever seen before. I mean, of course I have seen him grin. But maybe I was intrigued because I knew *why* he was grinning. You see, Losiah is Korean—100 percent Korean. Like 100. Not 99.99383 percent. No—100 percent. We know this because we adopted him from South Korea. I'm not Carmen Sandiego, but I'm certain that my six-month-old baby we picked up from the social service office on the south side of Seoul didn't just land there a week prior. Oh, and remember that DNA test that surprised me with my royal African roots? (I'm now taking my ancestors to mean that I am somehow related to a Nigerian prince, by the way.) When we got the results back, Heather and my daughters were freaking out looking at their percentages.

Heather's ethnicity estimate:
36% German
19% Irish
16% Mexican
9% Scottish

Sohaila's ethnicity estimate:
22% Mexican
14% Spanish
10% Basque (Huh?)
8% Nigerian

Seanna's ethnicity estimate:
20% Spanish
15% Mexican
14% German (Thanks, Heather)
10% Scottish
7% Nigerian

Losiah's ethnicity estimate:
100% Korean

We all laughed out loud when he read his. He was dying laughing. And it also was a reminder of just how much of a melting pot America is. Everybody has numerous ethnicities in them here. But it's easy to forget that is not the case in so many places across the planet, South Korea included.

So, herein I rest my case that my son is Korean. As if the case needed any more resting.

He wasn't smiling. It was almost a smirk. A smirk that had never been brought about by this feeling before, because he'd never had it. I realized in that moment that this was maybe the third time in his entire thirteen years of living with us that he had been surrounded by more people who looked like him than people who looked like us.

Now, we weren't going to South Korea; we were heading to Beijing, China. But that didn't matter. Most of the passengers on the plane looked way more like Losiah than they did the rest of us.

• • •

As we landed and entered Beijing, my son started walking with a swagger. He started walking at the front of the pack. People would speak to him in Mandarin. He would smile back and politely say, "English." But he just kept smiling.

He came alive in ways we had not seen before. It wasn't a massive shift, but it was a noticeable one. I don't know exactly what was going through his mind on a minute-by-minute basis, but my son suddenly swaggered since he was now the one who looked like everyone else and we were the different ones.

A while ago, someone at a kids' event called Losiah "flat face." When the teacher let me know, I was livid. I was ready to go find that kid and his parents and go give them an up-close-and-personal diversity, equity, and inclusion talk with a side of "Have your kid call my kid that one more time and let me show you what happens."

Fortunately for me, Losiah handled it like a champ. "They are probably having a hard family time at home, Daddy," he said. What sort of thirteen-year-old knows that those who end up wounding you are probably more wounded themselves? Apparently, my kid does.

But it wounded him, for sure. I knew what it felt like to be picked on in school because you look different from everyone else, but the difference here is that my son comes home and ends up looking different from everyone at home as well. It's deeper for him than I could ever understand, which is why this trip was bringing life out of him in ways I had not anticipated. He was being seen, but not in the way that most of us would assume that we would want to be seen.

You see, he was being seen as a part of something bigger. A part of a bigger culture. I think we can rush to assume that people just want to be seen for their individual accolades. For their skills. For their talents. But no. Sometimes being seen is more about simply belonging than anything else. Everyone wants to belong. And this trip was proving it.

On the last night of the trip, we decided to go to a Chinese cooking class. By this point, we had walked all over the neighborhood that our hotel was in and kind of felt like locals—in the most nonlocal way ever. You know the feeling, though: You have been in a place for seven days and suddenly you feel like you own the place just because you know where the best coffee in the hood is. That's how we were feeling that last night.

After the cooking class, I walked out to the corner of the intersection and began trying to hail a cab. One cab passed by empty. Another passed by empty. Another slowed down in front of us empty and then quickly sped off. Another passed by empty. I was starting to feel as though they weren't stopping for the foreigner. I was starting to get a wee bit perturbed. That was, until Losiah stepped in. He walked between me and the cars zipping by and said, "Dad, it's okay to feel different here. I'll hold your hand, and then everyone will know you belong."

And then he grabbed my hand while holding his other hand up like he had been hailing cabs his entire life. About two seconds later, a cab screeched to a halt right in front of us.

That smirk from the airport—it came back. We got in and the cabdriver drove us back to our hotel.

When we got out of the car, Losiah grabbed my hand again and walked proudly through the lobby as if to show the world that I was his and he was mine—which was true. He was seen.

He was seen by the strangers passing us on the sidewalks. He was seen by the cabdriver who decided that he was worth picking up even though I was not. He was seen by the concierge as we walked into the hotel.

He was seen in the ways that he wanted to be seen.

And that was all he needed.

• • •

As human beings, we are desperate to finally be seen. We want to be seen not only for *who* we are but also for *why* we are. Isn't that the truth?

This right here is the principle: Humans desire to be seen. We do. Everybody does. So that is where we are heading in this section. We have worked hard to learn how to simply *be*. Now let's start to *see*.

I want you to think about something for a second. Think about every person you have made eye contact with over the past two days. For some of you, that may be many. For others of you, that may not be anyone. But let me tell you something: Every single person you have seen is desperate to *know* that they are seen. Even if you do *see* them.

In other words, if they don't know that they are seen, then what good is it for them? To see another human is not only for your benefit but for theirs.

Almost all the ugliness that we encounter online can be boiled down to people wanting to be seen. Simply seen. I mean, let's talk about the fighting that we see in real life. Again, people wanting to be seen.

People marching at the Capitol? *See us.*

People protesting outside a school board meeting? *See us.*

People putting political signs in their yards? *See us.*

Once you see someone, you can't unsee them. And after the next few chapters, hopefully you will realize that seeing someone won't necessarily mean that you agree with them, but it will mean that you care about them.

I will fill you in as to how this part of how to human is essential not only for them but also for you. And I think that when you start to see the incredible impact *seeing* others has, you will start to practice this step more frequently than you ever imagined.

So let's get to opening the eyes in our heads and in our souls. It's time to see clearly.

8

· · ·

see bias

As 2020 marched on into early summer, it continued to mix civil unrest with Covid. Tensions escalated, as it seemed like every day there was *another* video of another unarmed Black person killed by police, and another ten thousand opinions as to how that officer or the victim could have handled it differently.

Conversations about race were becoming more and more heated and divisive. I tried my hardest to get people on the same page, but I realized something. The teachers, those of us in the Black community doing education online, were teaching from a place of our own personal stories and our being the victims of racism or racial bias—which works. My story has helped people understand that my reality as a Black man growing up in America was much different than the realities of most of those who follow me, and I think it helps people understand. But what that doesn't do is give clear action steps to help defeat a subconscious racial bias you may have or even help remove racist actions that you may not have ever seen as racist. This lack of clarity kind of defeats the purpose of educating.

Just getting people to understand something should never

be the goal. All that creates is conviction. As I stated in an earlier chapter, conviction without action is useless. Why would I want to create an army of people who simply care, if there is no action following their conviction? And that is what I was finding across the landscape of people who were willing to be allies but maybe didn't quite know how to get past their own bias.

So my strategy changed: How do we move to action?

. . .

I remember mulling this during the beginning stages of the protests over the murder of George Floyd. I remember thinking, *There must be more than just telling people that they need to go to a march. There must be more than simply telling people that they have subconscious bias inside them. What's another lesson I can create or teach to help them understand this?*

My DMs were filled with people asking what else they could do. How else could they be allies? And I had the shtick answers: Educate yourself. Own your privilege. Accept feedback. But as the summer began to creep up on us, as the tension in the air began to thicken like the humidity I was feeling when I walked outside my house in Nashville in early summer, I knew that the answer was certainly going to have to involve more than posting a black square on Instagram and not saying anything for a day. (Remember that trend?)* I think it was born out of a good heart, but as a Black man, what I didn't need my

---

* That one had me confused. The black-square-and-be-quiet thing. That's okay. I mean, I've been doing things my entire life that don't really make sense, but I do them anyway. Like folding my underwear when I don't care if it gets wrinkled. Like, why do I do that? It's weird. But I do it anyway. Back to not talking about my underwear . . .

White friends to do was just sit back and listen to Black people; I needed them to fight harder and speak louder than they ever had.

I felt like we went from *I can take action on my Instagram page* to *I can go to a march* to *holy crap, nothing is helping, the world is falling apart, and we are going to have a race war in ten days flat.* I specifically remember praying that God would give me the words to help my friends become more than sympathetic to my reality. I prayed that He would give me something for them, and of course, He always does. Maybe just not the way I want Him to answer.

I began a series of videos teaching my platform about the concept of racial bias and how we need to reject the notion that bias isn't in us and instead seek to find the bias and redirect it toward allowing us to grow. You've got to realize something here: Nobody, absolutely nobody, wants to imagine that they have any sort of bias inside them. Immediately, our minds go to the word *racist.* If I have bias, then I must be racist! But that's not the case. Having bias in you means that you are simply human. Bias is subconscious. It is grown in the corners of your heart. It's not something that you decide to have or be. It's not out front. It's not a membership card to bigotry. Bias is something that is a slow grow, and many of us have very good reasons to have grown these biases. Real-life experiences that have grown these biases in our hearts. Real life trauma that has slowly let out defense mechanisms that are created to protect our hearts. That's how many of our biases are born: out of protection of ourselves.

Not all our biases are born out of purely lived experiences. Some of them are certainly there because we know no better. We have seen television shows depict people of certain races certain ways, and if we are not living in a multicultural context, those biases can rapidly accelerate to become an everyday part of how we think.

So, when I was creating these videos, I wanted to make sure that everyone felt safe enough to experience them the way I wanted them to experience them: with firmness but also sincere grace. That's my mojo. It's the Carlos way. Love people toward change. "Kind" people toward change. I'm always trying to remind some super-fundamental Jesus people that Scripture tells us, "God's *kindness* is intended to lead you to repentance" (Romans 2:4, emphasis added). It doesn't say that it's God's *crushing* that leads to repentance. So that's the goal: *Kindly* show people the way to find their biases.

As I was working on this video series and researching different moments when bias came into play in historical situations, something insane happened. Like jaw-dropping racial-bias insanity that ended up being the basis for the change I want to see in others. Only I didn't see it in a movie. I didn't read it in a book. I didn't see it on the nightly news.

No.

I saw it in my front yard.

· · ·

When we moved into our neighborhood a few years back, I made friends with every single neighbor surrounding us. That's not really the case in many middle-class hoods in the States. People don't sit on their front porches anymore waving at those passing by. We use our homes as fortresses, where we hide out inside them instead of welcoming those who pass by. I know, I know. It's not *Leave It to Beaver* over here. I know that crime is up and that we must be diligent. I'm just saying that I don't know if we are doing this neighbor thing right. But that's for another book.

The first week we lived here, I walked over to Joe and Andy's house. They were so kind: "Anything you guys ever need, just come on over and ask." Sydney and James: "Oh my gosh, let's make sure to get our dogs together. Burley has been dying to have a friend to play with." I mean, I was scoring on the neighborly love charts right about then. Joy and Greg: "Why don't you bring Losiah over sometime to play some Ping-Pong?" And then I started walking across my yard to the house across the street to the west. But as I started crossing the street, an old man came walking out the door with a scowl on his face. It stopped me in my tracks. For more reasons than one, but the main reason being I didn't want to walk up on a grumpy old man with my super-bubbly self. *He must be having an off day. Maybe tomorrow I'll introduce myself.*

But tomorrow came and when he walked out to his mailbox, we locked eyes and I lifted my left arm and let out a "Hey, neighbor!" To which his eyes responded with a very sincere *I'm not into you, new neighbor. Please leave me alone.* At least that's what I saw. He walked back to his house, and I found myself staring. And then right before he opened the front door to his house, he quickly turned around as if he could feel me staring. It caught me off guard and I did that awkward thing we all do when we find ourselves staring at someone and then get busted. I quickly turned my head to the right and acted as if I weren't staring. But the funny thing about those moments is, *you know they know you were staring.* But we try to play it off anyway. (I mean, did I really think he thought I was just staring at a piece of grass for that long?)

Out of the corner of my eye as I was *not* awkwardly staring at a section of my lawn, I saw him walk inside his house and slam the door behind him. When he slammed the door, the American flag that was draped from the top of the front door to the bottom of the front door kind of halfway waved. The wind from the movement of the door highlighted the flag. And I suddenly could feel the blood rush to my face, like when the blood rushes to your face when you see something that makes you mad. But I didn't understand why the flag made me feel that way. It was as though it made me feel worse off than the crotchety old man himself did.

. . .

Now, hang with me for a second. Here is where I'm going to do some heavy lifting and you get to watch. I love America. I'm the son of a Black Panamanian from Colón, Panama, who immigrated to the United States of America in 1960 and was able to chase his dreams and achieve what many from his poverty-stricken city never have. This country has given so much to my family, so why in the world did my heart clench up in some sort of fist when I saw that flag wave at me?

I'll tell you why. Because subconsciously I had created a bias in my heart about the man across the street, and the flag cemented the bias in me. I had decided that the old man didn't like me because I was Black. And what did the flag have to do with any of that? Let me tell you.

Of the nine men who have called me the N-word since I've lived in Tennessee, *all of them* were old White men with an American flag framed across their chest, stitched to their hats, or splayed on their vehicle in some way, shape, or form. The flag hadn't wounded me, but those old White men displaying it had. And so, by process of association, I am triggered by those two things together.

Old White men and American flags.

So, I was thinking, *Sucks to be me, I know. I live across the street from a racist. This is going to be fun.*

My attempts to befriend him stopped at once. I would see this man every single day for the next four years and never say a word to him. There were times that we would find ourselves at our mailboxes at the exact same time and simply pretend the other wasn't there. *From ten feet apart.* There were times when we would be backing out of our driveways at the same time and one of us would have to let the other out before proceeding ourselves. There would be times that he would be taking his daily walk as Losiah and I were in the front yard kicking the soccer ball and we would continue to play this game of pretending the other neighbor simply did not exist. We have all had grumpy neighbors before, but have you had a blatantly racist neighbor?

And then in May 2020, right as I was creating those videos about racial bias for my community, God had the audacity to call me out on mine. *My* racial bias was toward old White men in the South. That's right. All the painful moments I had experienced at the hands of a racist old White man in the South had polluted the reality and truth that not all old White men from the South are racist. I knew this, but it didn't matter. That's the thing about bias: Knowledge in and of itself will never fix it. This statement was a major teaching point in my bias videos I was creating. You can't simply call the bias out of yourself; you must confront it. You must bust out of your bubble and surround yourself with the exact people you have a bias against. You must eat with them, shop with them, work with them. Yet there I sat making those videos while twenty-five feet from my basement sat a man whom I had a strong bias against. And remember, bias can be brought out from lived experiences. It's not like I didn't have a reason to believe what I did, but what I was about to find out was that our feelings don't always match up with reality.

You see, one morning as I was mowing my lawn, the racist old White man came walking out his front door. But this time, he had a can of paint. He started walking across his yard and toward my yard. *That's weird,* I thought. But then he stopped halfway across his lawn. He stopped right next to the statues of two bunnies. You know, like the stone statues of fairies and gnomes that your grandma has in her backyard. Except he had two white stone bunnies, probably about two feet tall. I don't think I ever really paid much attention to them. And so, racist, angry old White dude bent down next to one of the bunnies and opened his can of paint. He dipped the paintbrush into the can and pulled it out. The paint was black. *What in the world is this crazy old man doing?* And then he started to paint one of the white bunnies black. "Man, this dude is weirder than I initially thought" I said out loud as I raced by him on my fancy Cub Cadet lawn mower. He slowly and methodically continued painting it black. *It must be world-war-something-paint-your-bunny-black day,* I thought.

When he finished painting it black, he started to close the paint can. Why in the world wasn't he painting the other one black? What in the world? And then he slowly got up, at just about the speed you would imagine an old man would get up, and he walked back across his yard and toward his American-flag-draped front door. He walked inside and left that one black bunny to dry and me to think. Why did he paint only one bunny black? So I shut off the mower and ran inside. "Hey, babe! Heather! Come look at this," I told her. Heather followed me outside and simply said, "He did that to show what he believes about what's happening in the country right now."

"No way," I responded. "Not my racist, angry old White neighbor." I was shell-shocked. And I still didn't believe her hypothesis, but I had to find out. And you know what that was going to take? Me getting past my own issues and getting up close to his. It was the last thing I wanted to do, but I knew I had to. So the next morning, I woke up and sat on my porch. I knew exactly when the old racist guy walked out to get his paper every morning.*

And as sure as the sun rises and sets, there he came right on time, slowly shuffling his feet across his wet lawn. *Okay, Carlos. It's time. Go do it. C'mon, you got this.* I was having to psyche myself up to go ask him. I needed to know why he painted that bunny black. So I got up, walked down my three stone steps, and started walking across my lawn toward the man I'd lived across the street from for four years yet had never had a conversation with. When I got to the street, I shouted, "Hey, neighbor!" and he immediately turned his head toward me, scowling in harmony with my expectations. But instead of turning around, I kept walking toward him.

And you'll never believe what happened next.

• • •

You know, seeing people isn't always going to be comfortable. And the more I think about it, I don't believe it is supposed to be. What is comfortable is seeing the civilized and filtered version of people. The highlight reel. The version that they want you to see. Right? That's what we want to see. That's what

---

* Yes, he had an actual subscription to an actual newspaper. (Side note: Do Trans Ams still drive by your house at four in the morning with a guy named Biff throwing the paper out his sunroof?)

makes us feel better. Because seeing people for who they really are doesn't feel amazing. We end up at a loss of words. We end up not knowing how to handle the awkwardness of their current situation.

But can we once again look at how our role model of how to human did it? Jesus was not scared of being uncomfortable. He met people where they were despite the awkwardness of their situation. Can you imagine for a second if He showed up only to situations where things were a Pinterest-board collection of vibes?

That's not at all who Jesus was. He didn't just see the righteous and the ones that made the rest of society feel comfortable. It was quite the opposite. In fact, if we look closely at His life, we see that He *really* loved seeing a few groups of people that others didn't want to see.

Women. The poor. Oppressors. Racial enemies.

Women were normally given a community only as big as their family was. Men simply didn't speak to women. But not Jesus. He saw them. He spoke to them (see John 4:27). He equalized their status with men (see Luke 13:16). He ministered with them. He sent them to tell His good news (see Luke 24:1–11). You would be hard-pressed to convince me that Jesus treated men and women differently. He. Saw. Them.

Jesus humanized the poor. He saw them: "But when you give a banquet, invite the poor, the crippled, the lame, the blind, and you will be blessed. Although they cannot repay you, you will be repaid at the resurrection of the righteous" (Luke 14:13–14, NIV).

Jesus healed the racial divide. It's not a secret that Jews and Samaritans were not fond of each other. In John 4:4–42, Jesus ended up alone at a local watering hole with a Samaritan woman. They discussed some issues in differences between

Jewish and Samaritan worship while He simultaneously displayed obvious concern for the Samaritan woman.

> He himself is our peace, who has made the two groups one and has destroyed the barrier, the dividing wall of hostility, by setting aside in his flesh the law with its commands and regulations. His purpose was to create in himself one new humanity out of the two, thus making peace, and in one body to reconcile both of them to God through the cross, by which he put to death their hostility. (Ephesians 2:14–16, NIV)

When I read those sections of Scripture, I am immediately placed on alert. How am I treating the poor? How am I treating women? How am I trying to reconcile any racial bias in my own life?

It's heavy lifting, this seeing-people thing. I think the heaviest part is realizing *how we see* people. I wish I could just start this section off with "Just make sure everyone feels seen! That's all it takes!" but unfortunately we have to adjust the lenses on our own specs before people actually feel seen. We need to see *past* who we think people are and *into* who they *really* are. That's what Jesus did so well.

• • •

As I got closer to the old man's yard, my heart began to beat faster. If I ever needed to copy and paste what Jesus thought into my head, it was going to be at this very moment. I started recording on my phone in case things went south. And you'll never believe what came out of that racist, mean old man's mouth, because what happened next changed me.

9
• • •

see closer

"Hey, neighbor! My name's Carlos. I live across the street."
(As if he didn't know that. Sometimes we say the dumbest things when we are stressed out.)

"Well, hello there, neighbor," he said as the softest and most genuine smile sneaked across his freckled and sunspotted face. "My name is James, and I've only lived here since 1964." Still smiling. My heart simultaneously leaped and sank at the same time. *How is that possible?* you may wonder.

Well, let me tell you. At precisely the same moment, my heart was leaping for joy that I had just encountered such a soft-spoken yet clearly kind man while I was also hurling toward the abyss of shame that I had judged this man from fifteen feet away for years and years. But then my brain started doing its brain thing: *Don't get ahead of yourself, Carlos. Racists are nice too. Stop giving him the benefit of the doubt. Trust your bias; it's always true.* There it is. How often does this happen? We get surprised and knocked off our bias train but try our hardest to cling to the caboose before it races away.

I continued, "Well, I had to walk over here. I saw your bunny."

"Well, I saw your Santa Claus." He chuckled. He was obviously referring to my "Ho Ho HOPE" inflatable that I'd put up two months prior. What in the world had just happened? How did walking fifteen feet across the street suddenly flip my entire idea of who this was on its head? It wasn't done being flipped.

"No, but really, I saw you painting that bunny black, and I think I know why you did that, but I don't want to assume anything. Can you tell me why you painted that bunny black?"

Without missing a beat, the racist, old, White, American-flag-trooping man said, "Well, you know, with everything that's going on in the country today, with all the protests that are happening and everything that's happening with all the Black stuff, I figured this isn't a big way—I mean it's kind of small, to be honest—but this is my way of saying what I believe about this country. It's my way of saying that I believe your life matters."

Excuse me while I bend over to pick my jaw up off the floor. In the seven seconds it took for that old man to speak those words to me, four years of judgment, shaming, ignoring, and figuring all went out the window. Not only was this man *not* a racist man, but he was in fact the opposite. My mind was blown. Not because of anything he had done. Remember, he was just living his best retired life. No, it was because of what *I* had done. It was because of what my bias had placed on him.

He kept on: "You know, I could have painted both the bunnies black. I thought about it. But then it just felt right to paint this one bunny black. It's the bigger bunny. And I figured, George Floyd was six foot four, so I'll go ahead and paint the big one black."

Jaw back on the floor. How had I missed it? How had I missed the fact that this neighbor of mine was one of the kindest allies I had in this fight toward injustice? I know how I had missed it. I missed it because I hadn't truly *seen* him. I mean, I saw him every day. But was it truly him? Was it truly who God had created him to be? No. What I had been seeing was simply the figment of my imagination that I needed him to be. Was it that I wanted a villain to root against? Was it simply that I wanted to somehow feel like a hero? I don't know exactly why. We all have our reasons for placing things on other people that don't belong there, but what I did know was that everything was changing and I was so grateful.

• • •

James and I began to talk about his history in Nashville. About his love for our country. About his serving in the Vietnam War. About the fact that he's never been married. About how when he grew up in that house in the sixties, his parents had hired a Black woman to help around the house and essentially raise him.

"When I was a boy, my parents worked all the time. They were so busy working that they didn't have time to take care of the house and of me like they would have liked, so they hired a woman. She was a Black woman. And I can't imagine anyone looking at her any differently than they would look at me. She taught me how to brush my teeth. She taught me how to comb my hair. She helped me with my homework. She was basically like another mother. I wish I could do more, but painting this bunny seemed like the right thing to do."

A bunny. A freaking bunny. That's what had brought my bias crumbling down. About ten minutes into our conversation, I noticed that my phone was still recording the entire thing. Again, I was recording because that's just something that now I feel like I must do in these times. I hope that's not the case one day, but until it is, I will continue to hit record when I approach a situation that may go south. We bantered for a few more minutes until I felt a prompting of something I needed to say.

"James, so good meeting you. I just want to tell you something. I need to tell you I'm sorry. I'm sorry for ever thinking anything about you that wasn't true. I'm sorry for judging you. I'm trying to teach my platform about this thing called racial bias. That's basically what has happened here. When I see an older White gentleman like you, with an American flag on his door, I automatically assume that someone like you won't like someone like me. And I want to say I'm sorry, because that bunny is one of the most beautiful things I have ever seen."

He looked confused. Rightfully so. But then that soft smile returned, and he just kept on sharing stories about his life. I was mesmerized by his southern drawl and the cadence of his words, but I was equally fascinated that I—the one who was teaching fifty thousand people every day how to be less racist, which will in turn lead to being anti-racist—how I was just as in need of my lesson as everyone else.

We exchanged goodbyes, and I walked the fifteen feet back to my lawn and then went in the house.

"So? What did he say? Did he paint the bunny black because of why I told you he painted the bunny black?" Heather asked.*

* I'm not a statistician, but I'm fairly certain my wife is right 100 percent of the time. And it still bothers me.

"Yeah, babe. But you gotta listen for yourself." I played her the video, and she was just as in shock as I was.

I realized after showing her the video that I didn't need to go back to my basement to finish recording my teaching videos on racial bias. Four-point sermons need not apply for this lesson. I had the lesson in my hand. On my phone.

Remember when I asked God to give me something I could teach? Yeah. Thanks, God. This was more than I had expected. I ran out the door, across the street, and to James's front door. He met me after three knocks.

"Hey, man. I need to ask you something. I was recording our convo earlier today. I had forgotten I hit record once we started talking. I was recording just in case you were who I thought you were."

He smiled that crooked smile again.

"Could I upload that video to Instagram? I would love for my followers to see the bias inside me, and I think this teaches it so perfectly."

He cocked his head left.

It was in that moment that I realized I had used a few words for which James had no idea what I was talking about nor the new context in which those words exist.

Upload. Strike one. *Instagram.* Strike two. *Followers.* Strike three. Let me try again. "So, like the internet. I have a lot of people who watch videos that I make every day. Could I show them our convo?"

I pulled my phone out so he could watch it, but before I could hit play, he said, "Sure. That's neat." And he turned around to walk back to his recliner and the local news.

I smiled and sprinted back home. I uploaded the video, and two hours later it had been seen by more than a hundred thousand people. By the next morning, it had been seen over a million times and poor James was standing in my front yard being interviewed by our local news affiliate and then later in the week by *Access Hollywood*. The man was just enjoying his best retired life, when Carlos came along and ruined it all.

• • •

James and I have remained close friends. Now when I see him at the mailbox and he scowls at me, I know that's simply the way he does his face. You know? He's just relaxing his brow. And I also learned he is a little hard of hearing. He probably couldn't hear me half the time I was talking to him, and there I was, judging him. We talk about the weather. We talk about construction in our neighborhood. He talks about how he doesn't like them digging in our front yard to lay the new AT&T fiber, and I talk about how much faster the internet will be. He is a delight, and I'm so grateful to know him.

To put some nuts and bolts on this encounter, I would love for us to take a look at how we can break through our bias and *see* people and how seeing them will help not only them but us.

It's so hard to see people through our opinions and emotions these days. It almost takes superhuman strength to do it. Here's how we can put this in everyday terms. First, let's rewind to the man with the plan again: Jesus. But this time let's look at how He had set up His disciples (His homeboys) to pull this off without Him.

You see, when Jesus left the earth, He left what He called the Holy Spirit. That's who continues to speak to us even today!

And there is an incredible story of one of Jesus's disciples having to get uncomfortable in order to see some bias destroyed. Philip was one of Jesus's disciples. Read this story about him:

An angel of the Lord said to Philip, "Rise and go toward the south to the road that goes down from Jerusalem to Gaza." This is a desert place. And he rose and went. And there was an Ethiopian, a eunuch, a court official of Candace, queen of the Ethiopians, who was in charge of all her treasure. He had come to Jerusalem to worship and was returning, seated in his chariot, and he was reading the prophet Isaiah. And the Spirit said to Philip, "Go over and join this chariot." So Philip ran to him and heard him reading Isaiah the prophet and asked, "Do you understand what you are reading?" And he said, "How can I, unless someone guides me?" And he invited Philip to come up and sit with him. Now the passage of the Scripture that he was reading was this:

> "Like a sheep he was led to the slaughter
> and like a lamb before its shearer is silent,
> so he opens not his mouth.
> In his humiliation justice was denied him.
> Who can describe his generation?
> For his life is taken away from the earth."

And the eunuch said to Philip, "About whom, I ask you, does the prophet say this, about himself or about someone else?" Then Philip opened his mouth, and beginning with this Scripture he told him the good news about Jesus. (Acts 8:26–35, ESV)

Probably the most important facet of this passage is a simple historical one. This man in the chariot was different from Philip's society in a couple of big ways. First of all, he was Ethiopian, a completely different race than Philip was. Second, he was a eunuch, which meant he served on the Ethiopian queen's high court. To be a eunuch meant that you were castrated. Yup, that's right. You were castrated so that the queen knew you had a single focus in serving her. No other desires but serving her. This is an, ahem, extreme sort of dedication, but what I want us to get out of this was that this man was sexually different in that society. There were layers of extra complexity for Philip to relate to this man.

But the first thing that we see is that Philip was told by God to get up off his lazy butt and head out the door to a road in the desert. I don't want us to miss this part. I don't know what Philip was doing at the time, but he was home. And then God showed up and messed up the plans. It's never convenient to *see* other people when God asks us to, but alas, here we are. So, first he heard from God and then he went *Okay*.

This isn't complicated stuff. You either listen to your gut or you listen to God. You trust something bigger than yourself. I'm not going to get in the weeds of theology here, but just so you know where I'm coming from, I fully believe that we can hear from God. I believe He still speaks. And so that's where I'm going with this big piece of how to human. Once Philip got to the road, he saw this chariot with someone Philip didn't normally hang out with. Maybe Philip saw the Ethiopian and then looked past that chariot, hoping with everything that there was another chariot coming by with a Jewish man or something. Nope. Of course not.

Now, here is where most of us would feel like we had accomplished seeing someone. We would make eye contact and smile and wave and maybe give them a fist bump to the chest like, *I see you, bro. I got you,* and feel as though we had done our duty. Maybe Philip was feeling that. Maybe he even gave him the head tilt. (You know the one you give to someone when you're trying to be a little cool. Yeah. That one.) But then the scripture goes on. It says that God told him to go over *to* the chariot. It's getting tough, right? Like, *I get it, God. You want me to let people driving chariots know that I still see them. That I still love them.* Sure, that's easy. Right? Black square on Instagram. Retweet something someone else wrote. But to go up to the chariot? I promise you that Philip was *not* into that idea. Like I said, the eunuch was not someone people hung out with. But alas, Philip went up to the chariot. And then here comes the kicker. Ready?

> "Do you understand what you are reading?" And he said, "How can I, unless someone guides me?" And he invited Philip to come up and sit with him. (verses 30–31, ESV)

Did you catch that? Not only did Philip go to the road where the chariot was—the chariot that he maybe didn't want to be associated with—but then the Ethiopian asked him to get in the chariot. *To get in the freaking chariot.* Are you with me, fellow humans? It's not going to be enough to simply walk up to the chariots that we are uncomfortable with. No. We have to suck it up, place our opinions and agendas and egos aside, and get in their chariot.

And here's the deal: You're not always going to end up having a chariot experience like I had with James. I mean, that was an amazing chariot-I-didn't-want-to-get-in experience. The same thing happened with Philip. He got in the chariot and became boys with that eunuch. That's not going to happen all the time. But we aren't called to become best friends with the chariot occupants; we are simply called to *see* them. To let them know that they are seen.

So, what are the chariots that you need to go to the road to see? What are the chariots that you need to walk up to? What are the chariots that you need to get into?

Stay with me. There will be some chariots that you won't agree with a single bumper sticker those chariots have on them. You may disagree with everything those chariots stand for. That's great. I would hope that you have strong convictions. But don't for a second think that disqualifies you from getting in the chariot. You are getting in the chariot to let the person in it know that you *see* them, not that you agree with them.

• • •

Conservative chariots.

Liberal chariots.

Blue Lives Matter chariots.

Black Lives Matter chariots.

LGBTQ chariots.

Pro-life chariots.

There are so many chariots that we won't even get near because, *What if someone sees me near that chariot? Will they think I agree with that chariot?* I have good news for you: We aren't called to convince people who judge us from the sidelines of what our convictions are. We are called to simply go to the road, walk up to the chariot, get in it, and let the people inside know that they are seen and loved.

That doesn't mean that you turn your back on your convictions. It's the opposite. It shows the person you are in front of that *in spite* of your convictions, you *see* them while still holding to your convictions.

That's it.

See them.

Getting off my sofa, walking to the road, walking up to James's chariot, and then getting in it was not what I desired to do that day, but boy am I glad I did.

Seeing humans isn't easy, but it's what we need to do to continue to course-correct humanity. I'm certain of that.

So, after we see our bias, we get to see people for who they really are. And in this case, seeing is believing. But only from up close. Really, really, *really* close. Like inside-their-chariot close.

So go on. You got this. Your chariot awaits.

10

. . .

see to serve

The danger in sharing the lesson I shared in the previous chapter is that it can become an excuse as opposed to an encouragement. Very quickly. You see, as I saw the black-bunny video shared over and over again, as it picked up steam in the media, I began to see myself tagged with a different message than the one I had hoped would get shared. Not by everyone, but a new message was beginning to emerge that was accompanying my video. The message went from "We all have bias, so let's acknowledge it and work on eliminating it" to "Look, here is a video of a Black man who says he has racial bias toward White men. Black people are racist too." It behooves me to say (I've always wanted a reason to say that) that I went at this narrative faster than Usain Bolt in 2010. I quickly uploaded another story correcting this plot twist.

"Dear 2.3 million people who viewed the black-bunny video. The point of the video wasn't to make you feel better about your own bias. The point was to show you that you—yes, even you—must face it and destroy it. And the destruction takes place through forgiveness. Not your forgiveness, but theirs." And I quickly hit upload. About a fourth of my newly garnered ten thousand followers walked out the Instafamilia door as quickly as they'd walked in.

For the next two months and deeper into the summer, I noticed that the pace at which people were seeking out how to deepen their understanding of racial reconciliation began to slow. That's to be expected. If there's one thing I have preached the past few years till I was out of words, it's that our souls and psyches were not created to consume the amount of content we consume. We weren't created to carry it. So after a summer of riots and shootings and learning, it seemed only normal that some of the pace of education lessened. But Lord have mercy if 2020 wasn't replacing one traumatic event for another.

Let's just jump to a month after the black-bunny incident for a little recap.

Do you have your therapist's phone number on speed dial? After the next minute, you may want to call them. Just typing this out is giving me some major anxiety.

June 30: Following a vote by the state legislature, Mississippi Governor Tate Reeves signs a bill that retires the official state flag—the last state flag incorporating the Confederate battle flag in its design.

July 10: The number of confirmed Covid-19 cases in the United States exceeds three million.

July 10: California officials announce that as many as eight thousand prisoners could be released ahead of schedule in an unprecedented attempt to stop the spread of the coronavirus inside state prisons.

July 14: The Trump administration orders hospitals to bypass the Centers for Disease Control and Prevention (CDC) and send all Covid-19 patient information to a central database in Washington.

July 22: President Trump announces a surge of federal officers into Democratic-run cities following a federal crackdown on protests in Portland, Oregon.

July 30: President Trump suggests the 2020 presidential election be delayed, saying increased voting by mail could lead to fraud.

August 2: Firefighters continue to battle the Apple Fire in California, which burned twenty thousand acres in Cherry Valley and surrounding areas of Riverside and San Bernardino counties, destroying one home and prompting evacuations of thousands of others.

August 16: Thunderstorms trigger hundreds of wildfires in California, prompting evacuations as a record-breaking heat wave taxes the state's power grid.

August 16: The SCU Lightning Complex fires start, affecting several San Francisco Bay Area counties. Almost four hundred thousand acres are burned, making it the third-largest wildfire in California history at that time.

August 16: The August Complex fire starts in Northern California. By September 9, it becomes the largest fire in California history, burning more than one million acres.

August 16: Death Valley hits 130 degrees, thought to be the highest temperature on earth in nearly a century.

August 23: Protests break out in Kenosha, Wisconsin, after the shooting of twenty-nine-year-old Jacob Blake by a police officer.

August 25: Two people are shot and killed during Wisconsin unrest. A suspect is arrested. Soon after, professional athletes start to boycott their sports to protest the shooting of Jacob Blake.

I'll go ahead and wait for you to finish that call with your therapist. I'll wait. No, seriously. I mean, what a stretch of eight weeks! That was just a blip of difficulty in the middle of the toughest year many of us had ever had. Add on top of that, we were all trying to dodge this invisible virus that was slowly but surely inching closer and closer to every single one of us. At this point, we almost all knew someone who had gotten Covid, and we were holding our breath, hoping it would pass sooner rather than later. And not only were we dodging a virus, but many of our California friends and family were dodging wildfires.

· · ·

My family and I were in Kalispell, Montana, where I was officiating at my friend Liz's wedding. It was gorgeous. It was my birthday weekend, and I couldn't think of anywhere better to be than with my friends in Montana.

When I walked in from the rehearsal on the lake lawn at the lodge, I saw a look on Heather's face that made me lose the blood flow to my head for a moment. It's that look where you know that someone has died. But she was on the phone saying, "Mmm hmm. Yeah. Okay," repeatedly, so I knew she was listening intently to whoever was telling her the bad news. Who was it? Was it Nani? Was it Rick? My mind was spinning in the ten seconds it took her to finish the conversation. When she hung up, I aggressively asked, "Well? What's wrong? What's happening?" She just sat there, her lip trembling, with a tear forming on the inside of her left eye. "Nobody died. It's my parents. The fire has turned south and is headed directly to Prather. Straight down the four lanes. They have to get out now."

I didn't say anything for a second. I let the news sink in. After this already horrible year? Where her parents own a tiny local pizza restaurant at the base of the Sierras, in a foothill town called Prather, in a year where they have already lost so much income, so much of their business? Now they are going to lose their farm, their house, their livestock? It didn't seem fair. I snapped out of it.

"Babe, okay. What can we do? Do you want to fly there? Do you need to go? How can we help?"

And I did what I had done time and time again. It had been a while since I'd called upon the collective strength of my Instagram family, and I was a little gun-shy to ask for anything after so many of the people who had prayed for my baby girl in the hospital took back their prayers after I began speaking up for injustice. After I became more of who I was created to be. I didn't want to ask for help and have people put an asterisk on their support. I didn't want to feel like I had to tone down my message to get some help. Because let me tell you something about how 2020 made me begin to think. I knew that even though I was educating in grace-filled ways, there were still people who were simply against the message in general. They didn't think that racism was a problem in America. They didn't think that anything needed to be done differently in policing for progress to be made. They didn't think that there were any broken systems. And although I had loved those who thought differently than I, although I had listened and debated and maintained relationships with many who saw the world differently than I, in this part of California, it wouldn't be a stretch to say that most people here looked at America through a wee different lens than I did. And of course they would. They weren't living in my reality in the South. They hadn't lived my same experiences. So why would I imagine they would see things as I did? But in this moment of crisis, in a moment where I needed them, I was scared that if I asked, it would fall upon deaf ears because of my political ideas. And that broke my heart. That people would decide not to help based on some things I believed that had nothing to do with this situation. Now knowing that I have just as many conservatives that follow me as I do liberals, I'm going to get a little more vulnerable here. I'd say the reason most people were listening and learning from me is because what I was teaching about racial reconciliation was not about left or right; it was about being human. I don't know any Republicans personally who are racist. I don't know any Democrats personally who are Marxist. But man, doesn't the world want us to believe the worst about each other?

Yes, the world does, but the worst is not true. We are all much more alike than we could imagine. So even though most people exist somewhere left or right of the center, it was hard for me, because the ones I had served the longest, the ones I had stood in front of week after week after week, the evangelical church, were the ones slowly but surely distancing themselves from me. I was getting more and more opportunities to speak to corporate clients on diversity and equality than to the church. It was blowing my mind that Christians were the ones who were distancing themselves from my message yet the world was wanting to get better and heal the racial divide. It was breaking my heart and continues to break it to this day. Shouldn't it be the other way around? Shouldn't the church be who's leading the charge toward racial reconciliation? I digress. TED Talk over.

I started scrolling through my Facebook friends who lived in this area of California. Slowly but surely, I realized that almost all of them had either blocked me or unfriended me. *No.*

Way. My nightmare was being realized. There was one guy in particular whom I knew had the capacity to help my in-laws, but I knew that he stopped seeing eye to eye with me a while ago and it wasn't worth it to even ask.

So instead I shot a flare into the California social media sky and asked if anyone had the capacity to get a horse trailer up to my in-laws' property to evacuate their animals and help them get out.

Within five minutes—five minutes!—I got a Facebook message from this guy: "Hey, Carlos. I'm so sorry about your in-laws. I'd love to help. Here's my number. Just call me and let me know how I can help."

I cried. It turned into an ugly cry for about four seconds. Nobody saw it. I walked into the bathroom of our hotel room and looked in the mirror and let out a quick sob. Why did his message hit me like that? I think it was a culmination of many things. I think it was the sheer exhaustion of 2020 crashing wave after wave of trauma over me. I think it was the fatigue of wanting to walk on eggshells while simultaneously not walking on eggshells to help guide people correctly in this toxic season of social media. I think it was seeing someone who quietly left me online just as quietly come back in to help. Once again. Back to the first story of this entire book. At the end, we all are going after the same thing: We just want to help people. And for that man to *see* me in this moment, it meant the world, because he was seeing more than me when he saw me; he was seeing my family, my wife. And it made me cry.

. . .

We are in desperate need of seeing each other despite our divisive opinions. I'm going to get more into that in the next chapter, but suffice it to say that this guy couldn't get all the way to their house. For me, it didn't matter. It was truly the attempt to help that healed my heart in a way that I didn't even know it needed. I had toughened up my heart so much in the previous months of 2020 that I didn't even know how thick the callus was until in this moment it was quickly ripped off and I felt. I simply felt when I didn't know I needed to feel.

I felt seen when I was served.

I think of the service industry. We would all like to believe that when we sit down at a restaurant that we have never been to, the server who approaches our table is going to serve us no matter what our deeply held beliefs are. Right? These days, even *that* is getting harder and harder to pull off. But in a human-forward world, this is what we have come to expect.

My server doesn't know how much I'm paying in taxes a year. They don't know how I treat my friends. They simply serve because they have been called to (or hired to, but you get it). And when you get great service, you feel seen. Now, take that to the extent of when people serve you who aren't paid to serve you. YOU FEEL SEEN. It takes the phrase "It's the thought that counts" and puts teeth to it.

Jesus, our "How to Human" guide, came to serve. That was His modus operandi. Here's what He told His disciples in Mark 10.

> You know that those who are regarded as rulers of the Gentiles dominate them, and their men of high positions exercise power over them. But it must not be like that among you. On the contrary, whoever wants to become great among you must be your servant, and whoever wants to be first among you must be a slave to all. For even the

Son of Man did not come to be served, but to serve, and to give His life—a ransom for many. (verses 42–45)

He came not to be served but to serve.

I mean, we could end the book right here. This is the secret sauce.

You know it's true. When someone serves you because it's just in them as opposed to someone made them, you feel seen. We don't have to dissect the Greek to get to the heartbeat of this story. It's right there in front of us.

It's why my wife feels way more loved when I randomly do the dishes that have been piled up even though it's the kids' responsibility but they have already gone to bed. When she wakes up in the morning fully expecting to have to walk into the kitchen and clean it from the night before but I've stepped in and served her, she feels so loved. Because she feels seen.

I could take her to dinner and a movie and spend $75 (probably more like $130 these days) and she would not feel nearly as seen as when I did those dishes.

So, let's take that charge by Jesus seriously. How can we serve those around us today? I mean, let's get *real* sticky here, like ground-level actions:

1. *Donate.* I'm not talking about big bucks here. Just donating $1.50 is something most of us can do. Not all of us, but most of us. So, if you have $1.50 right now, go find an org that will let you drop them a small donation and do it.

2. *Help feed the hungry.* There is an organization near Nashville called One Generation Away. They are a nonprofit that seeks to eliminate food insecurity by bringing healthy food to people in need. The United States throws away 30

percent of good food *a day*. That's right. So, what One Generation Away does is go rescue that food from grocery stores and restaurants. They put the food in a freezer truck, and then on the weekends you can volunteer to help pass out these fresh groceries that would normally go bad. I was able to serve on a Saturday, and it was breath to my lungs.

3. *Volunteer your services.* You have a skill. You know you do. Now, you may not think that it's worthy of giving away, but I promise it is. Can you use a hammer without injuring yourself? Give Habitat for Humanity a call. Are you a budgeting ninja? Call Boys and Girls Club and offer to teach young men and women to budget. Do your friends tell you that you talk too much? Go to a retirement home and talk with people who have long been forgotten.

These are just three simple ways that you can help make a change *this week*. There are people and organizations that need to be seen not when you finish this book but now. So when you end this chapter in ten seconds, open your phone and find people and places that need you to see them and serve them.

(Sorry 'bout them toes. I'm gonna keep stepping on 'em.)

Try it. Today. And see how much more human you feel.

11

. . .

see clearly

Much of the tension that was bubbling up through the cracks in the surface of society in late summer 2020 was being forced to the surface not by differing opinions but by a sheer lack of attempts to see one another clearly.

People were losing their minds over if someone wore a mask or not. Like *literal minds were lost* and we are still looking for them today. I'm not saying I don't think that subject matter was important, but I just think in the future, people studying history are going to look back at relationships that ended over a mask and they will think we were insane. Not insane because we had debates over the usefulness or lack of usefulness of masks but that we were so hard-pressed to not back down from our opinions on the issue that we ended up losing relationships over it. Masks were and are (as of the time of this writing) a big deal. But I cannot fathom they should be a big enough deal to ruin relationships just because we refuse to see the other person's point of view clearly. Something in us just can't seem to do that.

Let's move to another issue: no-knock warrants. After the

death of Breonna Taylor, everybody had an opinion about what happened. And although it was about a certain subset of laws within law enforcement, it turned quickly into being pro-police or anti-police. And the faster the conversation grew, the faster the two sides spread apart. Before you knew it, it was *defund the police* versus *bring armored tanks into every neighborhood.* Okay, maybe it wasn't *that* extreme, but it did get complicated quickly. People on both sides of the issue were not really interested in seeing the other person's side; they just wanted to continue to build the case supporting their own opinion. And this isn't just a 2020 problem. This is, at the core, a problem with dialogue. We no longer can have crucial conversations in which people can disagree without the result being hating each other. It's not supposed to be this way, but here we are.

I had *very* strong opinions about the Breonna Taylor case and no-knock warrants in the South. I researched where they came from, and knowing how much racism played a part in so much of our policing throughout the history of our country, I was steadfast in my opinion that I wanted them gone.

I made videos supporting my case. I wrote articles picking apart someone defending no-knock warrants. I watched recordings from police officers who were for getting rid of them and I shared those recordings as well.

But you know what I was *not* doing? Listening. I was not listening to people in support of no-knock warrants to see clearly; I was listening only to build my case. And I had a solid one. But you know what is hilarious? I had a friend in law enforcement in Southern California who served no-knock warrants monthly. Okay, so maybe I need to change the descriptor in the sentence above from hilarious to tragic, because it was tragic. It was tragic that in all my research, in all my study on no-knock warrants, in all my teaching, I had never even asked him about them. And it made me realize that maybe I wanted to *feel* right more than I wanted to *be* right.

Now, before I continue on, I need to let you know that issues we are passionate about are extremely important. I mean, many of them are a matter of life and death. I don't want you to think I am trivializing them. I'm not. But we need to consider the value of getting closer to those who may doubt you. Those who may doubt the very essence of everything you are about. I realized that I had turned the issue of no-knock warrants into just that: an issue. But the truth is that every single issue we are passionate about is not just an issue; it's not just a hot topic. Speaking of hot topics, I love what my friend Kailey Dickerson says on her podcast: "If you want a Hot Topic, go to the mall." I laughed out loud the first time she told me that. Me, on the other hand—I'm all about the hot topics. Maybe because my mom never let me shop there when I was a kid. She said it was an evil store. I just wanted to get a poster of Tiffani Amber Thiessen for my locker. I digress.

Here I was, super-passionate about no-knock warrants, yet I'd never asked my friend who serves them as part of his job his thoughts. So I opened Marco Polo and shot him a message. (Now, if you are reading this in like 2090 and have no idea what Marco Polo is, it was an app on your phone where you could send video messages to each other. I know that by now, in your time, you are probably beaming from country to country by reducing your DNA to molecular levels and then rebuilding them somewhere else on the planet, but listen here: All we have are these phones in our hands. That's as close as it gets to being able to beam from one land to another.)

Hey, Eric. Obviously, you follow me on Instagram and know how I feel about the issues of no-knock warrants.

Could you give me your experience with them? I want to make sure that I talk to you about them before I continue building my case against them. 'Cause you know where they came from here in the South? They came as a way to specifically continue to target and monitor Black people to oppress them. I have facts. I have data. So just know where I'm coming from, okay?

I hit Send.

• • •

I was a little nervous as the message whooshed off. You see, Eric and I had already gone back and forth on some subjects that we were passionately disagreeing about. And it sucked, because I don't think we had ever really disagreed on things in the past. Or I was beginning to realize that maybe we just didn't know that we disagreed on things in the past, because we obviously did. And that's the case with all of 2020. We suddenly knew opinions that our close friends and family had that maybe we were never supposed to know in the first place.

Eric shot back a video message quickly. To be honest, I thought it was going to take him a few days to gather his thoughts. Nope. It was almost as if he were waiting for me to send him that video.

I hovered my finger over the play button on the screen. I had two thoughts in my head, the first being that I didn't know if I had time to adequately digest the thesis on why no-knock warrants were good. I also hate leaving videos watched but not having enough time to send a response back. The second thought I was having was that I didn't want to be proved wrong. Can I get a witness? We love having one-way conversations these days—which aren't conversations. We want them to feel as though they are, because we put something out on social media and then pick and choose a few comments to interact with. But in reality, that isn't human conversation. Not that a video message is perfect, but it allows for more conversation than a static post does. And I didn't want to hear something that could sway me or change my mind. Isn't. That. Something?

After mulling over my thoughts for a few minutes, I clicked Play.

"Hey, man. I'll get back to you when I have some time."

I laughed out loud.

The next day, Eric had some time.

"Hey, man. You love me, right?" he started. And I was a little put off by his question. Just because I loved him didn't mean I was going to agree with him. Who did he think I was? Of course I loved him. But I still thought no-knock warrants should be abolished. He continued,

I know you love me. And I want you to hear me when I tell you that I love you too. I love that you are passionate about these things. But I want you to hear me when I tell you that I think you are wrong on this one. Listen, every time I have to go serve a no-knock warrant, it's normally for some real, *real* bad dudes. Like the kind of dudes that *want* me to knock, because they probably have been tipped off that I am coming, and they are just waiting for the knock. They are waiting to pump a whole bunch of lead through the thin door that they find themselves hiding behind. So when I knock, that's their plan. And when I must go serve a no-knock, it's normally in the middle of the night. So I make sure to kiss Lori goodbye. I make sure to kiss Rami goodbye. I make sure to kiss Cameron goodbye. And I kiss them goodbye because I don't know how the search warrant is going to go down. And so I have a question for you: When I show up to the bad guy's house, do you want me, your friend Eric, to knock and let the bad guys know that I am there? 'Cause if I do, then things go south fast. We are granted no-knock warrants for a reason, and that reason is so that after I clock out, I can go back home and kiss my family again.

The video ended, and his face froze on my screen. His face was so close to mine in that moment. Not in a creepy way; it just felt so much closer than when the video started.

Of course I want Eric to go kiss his family again, because I love them too. And suddenly I began to see things much more clearly.

Like when my grandpa reads the newspaper. He holds his coffee mug and that paper about three inches from his pie-hole. Why? Why is the paper so near his face? *So he can see.* It's not rocket science. It's why microscopes are used in science. It's why telescopes are used by astronomers. It's why magnifying glasses are used by five-year-old boys to burn up ants. Okay, maybe not that last one, but you get my point. We must come near. We must continue to look up close at things that we feel strongly about. It clears things up.

Now, does being near to something we disagree with mean that we are going to suddenly have an about-face on our convictions and opinions? Absolutely not. If anything, it may clearly affirm that you were right all along. But dare I say that you can't be clear about something if you do not get close. It's essential.

Take this situation with my friend Eric and no-knock warrants. Did it change my mind about them? A little. Not all the way. But I was able to put skin on this issue because I saw it from a much closer perspective than I ever did before. I realized that maybe not *all* no-knock warrants should be done away with. There are still bad people in this world, and those bad people are waiting to do bad things to the good people who are trying to stop them. And maybe for them, we need no-knock warrants. Or maybe I was just thinking that my friend Eric should be the only cop to be able to use them. But along with those shifting feelings, I also knew that many no-knock warrants in the South are not being used correctly and that the system they are used under needs a major renovation. I strongly agree with that, but I never would have been able to process this way had I not gone near the human who held opposing views to mine.

• • •

We've got to get near so we can be clear. We have put such distance between ourselves and people we used to do life with. And in many cases, that is needed. Nobody needs to be near someone who is bad for their mental health. But there are people who are doubting you loudly that you would rather not hang with simply because it's going to take a lot of work, right? Let's stay away from them. The ones who loudly oppose you. Stay away, right?

I don't know.

Let's go back to our model: Jesus.

If there was a man who did *not* keep His distance, it was Jesus. The man was *near,* all the time. He walked toward those who disagreed with His point of view. He dined with those who laughed at His ideas. Even His own disciples were some of His greatest doubters.

Let's take this moment when He pulled off what He promised them would happen: He came back to life.

Watch this:

The 11 disciples traveled to Galilee, to the mountain where Jesus had directed them. When they saw Him, they worshiped, but some doubted. Then Jesus came near. (Matthew 28:16–18)

I absolutely love this passage. Jesus showed up where He told the disciples to meet Him after He casually rose from the dead. There they were, waiting on Him to show up, and poof, Jesus did a Jesus thing and appeared. Some did what He expected them to: They worshipped Him. I mean, how could you not at that point? Well, just ask the rest of them, *because it says they doubted.* And how could you not? Listen, I've never had someone I know resurrect themselves and then show up on a hike, so I can't tell you exactly what I would do, but I would probably be leaning toward the "some doubted" camp. Right? I can just imagine their convo: "Yo, Matthew! No way. No freaking way that's Him. I don't believe it." That's what I would be shouting.

And I love that it doesn't say that Jesus pulled out His phone (I mean, He didn't have one, of course—you're welcome for that theological nugget) and started reading the disciples articles about how it really was Him. He didn't send them to the local synagogue to go read up on some of the Old Testament prophets who prophesied that this was going to happen. He didn't try to prove His point in all the ways we like to prove our points from afar. He simply did one thing, the most human thing that He could do. Scripture says that "Jesus came near" (verse 18).

He *came near,* for what better way was there to show them that it was truly Him? What better way to erase their doubts that He'd done what He said He was gonna do? There was no better way.

He got near. They saw clear. That's it, fam.

We've got to continue getting near to the people we are doubting or are doubting us. It's the most human thing you can do. It doesn't take a degree in debate. It doesn't take a master's in whatever subject matter you are doubting or being doubted on. All it takes is your two feet. Put one in front of the other and start getting near some people who you haven't been near to in a very long time. There can be no healing if there is no feeling. And I'm talking about that up close feeling. Feeling near. It's how we can see clearly again.

The hard part is not going to be physically walking near them; the hard part is going to be walking toward them in your heart. I get it. But let's look at some ways to do that. I specifically try to find people who believe differently than I do when it comes to their faith. It not only helps me build empathy, but it allows me to listen to understand, not to reply. It allows me to learn and educate myself on their point of view. Just because you spend time with your Muslim friend actually *learning* about them doesn't mean you are *becoming* Muslim, but what it will do is allow you to come near them.

What about the really fuel-filled friendships? The ones that political difference has slowly separated? It could be as simple as grabbing your phone right now and shooting the person a text. You can literally copy and paste the following. (Just change the name, unless your friend is, uh, named Brady too.) "Hey, Brady! I really miss you, friend. Want to head to a movie next week?"

See, a movie allows you to be close without having to make small talk the entire time. A sporting event is the same. I actually love the sporting event idea because it allows you both to cheer for the same thing, and honestly that's what this whole thing is about. There are other ways to do this, but you already know that. And you know who it is you need to simply get near to.

To take the next step in seeing humans, we must close that gap. Then the rest of this human thing will begin to align to the place where people are finding freedom again. Be. See. Free.

It's almost time to set ourselves and others free. But we have one more step in this seeing section, and it's going to take everything inside you to pull off. Ready? Meet me in the next chapter once you've decided who you are going to see clearly again.

12

• • •

see journeys

As fall 2020 approached, many of us began to take inventory of everything that had been stripped away. We went from being scared to being angry to figuring out what the next thing we were going to rage about was. The year had conditioned us to look for things to freak out about. And it wasn't slowing down. As the fall approached and many people were getting tired of others telling them what they could and couldn't do, where they could and couldn't eat, where they could and couldn't travel to, we were now being inundated with messages on who we should and shouldn't vote for.

Have I told you already how perfect of a storm 2020 was to knock us off course as humanity? I'm here to remind you of that statement. It was all so much. And our pandemic-rookie selves were a hot mess.

I had a horrible feeling about what the next few months of this presidential-election cycle was going to do to us. Could we take another blow? A pandemic, racial unrest, and a presidential election?

Hopefully by now, you realize that I am the most glass-half-full guy in the bunch. There is nobody more glass-half-full than me. And at that point in the year, I was beginning to think that the glass was not only empty but also on the verge of shattering.

After my conversation with my buddy Eric, I decided to take inventory of my relationships—not necessarily of my acquaintances, but of my actual friends. Now, I'll let you know that I'm not the greatest friend on the planet. I'm not a horrible friend, but I'm just not the type you would want to model friendship after. I reply to text messages three days later; I borrow things and forget that I borrowed them for six months; I don't know when your birthday is. I'm that friend. But I'll also be the first person at the hospital if someone gets sick. I'll be the first one to call you if drama arises. I'll also pray nonstop for you and text you prayers daily until whatever crisis you find yourself in has been averted.

It's like my poor friends don't know what to do with me. I'm that one. So, as I was taking inventory of my friendships, it started me down a path of realizing that I simply needed to be a better friend. I simply needed to more often see my friends where they were. And although I had purposely distanced myself from Eric at one point to protect my own calloused heart from getting wounded, there were a few friends who I had not distanced myself from and yet they felt so distant. Weird.

Micah had been one of my best friends since our freshman year in college. I'll never forget this scrawny, mullet-wearing, red-pickup-driving country boy living across the hall from me that year. He was so aw-shucks jolly. You know what I'm talking about: a good ole boy. He made much more of an impact on me because I was one of only a few Black students on campus, and I already had my guard up and my super-friendly non-Black Black guy character ready for the show.

Let's just say that this good ole country boy ended up becoming one of my best friends. I would take a bullet for him. We have been friends for more than twenty years. Our kids grew up together. He was the first one to show up at my doorstep after my life fell apart in 2010. He has been there through every high and low in my adult life. And he lived ten minutes from me. That's why it was so weird when I realized that I hadn't heard from him in a few months. I know we were both busy. I had constant speaking engagements and was producing content for my online platform seven days a week, and he was a bigwig at some medical-solutions company, but why hadn't he called me in a few months? Notice I wasn't asking why I hadn't called him. That would be too difficult of a question to answer. I was about to text him when I thought I would see what he'd been up to on Instagram. He used to comment all the time on my posts, and I used to see his posts all the time. When I went to his profile, I noticed that he hadn't posted anything in a few weeks. *That's weird,* I thought. And then I saw something that shook me more than it probably should have. But it was 2020, so give me a pass. I saw at the top of his profile that he wasn't following me on Instagram! What in the world? Maybe he accidentally unfollowed me? Nah. That's like people saying that their Instagram got hacked. So, after releasing that ridiculous conspiracy theory that he accidentally unfollowed me, my heart sank. I knew that something was amiss.

"I'm so freaking tired of all this crap," I said. And I was. I was so tired of having to continue to rescue relationship after relationship. Things were so easy for so long, and then 2020 gave us ample opportunity to come apart. I knew what I needed to do, but I didn't want to do it.

• • •

There's a saying that I had been using repeatedly in 2020 to get people to understand from where I wanted them to approach a better understanding of race and the human condition. It's a phrase that has been tattooed on my heart for a while now. I first heard it from my friend Pastor Mike Ashcraft in Wilmington, North Carolina. It's a catchphrase that I used almost daily when people would ask me where I stood on an issue. Having something of a public profession, I get asked this all the time. In media interviews, in DMs, in conversations over a meal. "Carlos, where do you stand on this issue?" It could be about theology. It could be related to LGBTQ. It could be political issues. It could be related to race. Everyone always wants me to publicly state where I stand, and I have answered the exact same way ever since I heard Mike teach the reply to me years ago.

"Carlos, where do you stand on abortion?"
I reply, "I don't stand on issues; I walk with people."

"Carlos, where do you stand on LGBTQ rights?"
I reply, "I don't stand on issues; I walk with people."

"Carlos, where do you stand on the second amendment?"
I reply, "I don't stand on issues; I walk with people."

And it drives people crazy. But the reality of their question has little to do with me and everything to do with them. They want to be able to decide if I am worth following or listening to based on a single opinion that I have. And that is a dangerous place for them to exist, because you are setting yourself up to live in a bubble. By removing people's voices from your life because you disagree on a certain hot topic is shallow at best and toxic at worst.

And it's not that I'm avoiding the topic.

Take, for instance, LGBTQ rights. I've never publicly said one way or the other what I believe,* because that is a question that deserves dialogue. It moves forward relationally, on a person to person level. Reducing it to an issue is inappropriate because it is about people. My friends in the LGBTQ community know where I stand. My friends with LGTBQ family members know where I stand. And those are the people who get to know. Why? Because it's not about an issue; it's about people. When an issue stops becoming about an abstract idea and becomes about a person who can be listened to, known, and loved, *then* real work can be done. But to simply stand on a pedestal and shout out your opinion on an issue like that? There's really no point.

How about issues of race? Dear people, Morgan Freeman isn't your friend. Denzel Washington isn't your friend. Candace Owens isn't your friend. David Harris isn't your friend. These are a few Black voices who argue that systemic racism isn't an issue. And you have every right to learn from them.

You do! Seriously. I listen to them, and I learn about their point of view every day. Go for it.

But if you are listening to only them and not the Black people who are in your life *daily,* you're doing it wrong. So instead of hearing an argument from a big-name Black voice that confirms your opinion (assuming that it is your opinion) that racism isn't a big deal in America, ask your Black friends about

---

* Now, don't go googling right now. Stay focused. You won't find it out there. ☺

their experience with racism. And not your Black acquaintances; your Black *friends*.* Ask them about their experience with racism in America. Go ahead. Do it. Because I promise you that when you know someone who has experienced systemic or just plain old racism in America, it no longer is an issue you have an opinion on. Something happens. Something to make it real. Something that affects someone you love.

I'm not saying that I won't publicly state my opinion on things or that someone can't figure out what I believe by simply watching what I do, but I'm not going to give someone a reason not to learn from me without them even knowing me. I *do* let my opinions be heard on issues. But only when I'm walking alongside the real, live, flesh-and-blood people those issues affect.

So go ahead and steal the line. Use it as your own. Say it with me:

I don't stand on issues; I walk with people.

. . .

Back to my former friend who I was deleting from my phone because he unfollowed me on Instagram. After picking my wounded heart off the floor, I did what every responsible adult would do upon realizing that one of their best friends has stopped being friends with them: I ignored it.

He can find me if he ever wants a relationship again, I thought. I mean, I always knew that we probably saw a few things differently, but certainly not what I was talking about online. Certainly not.

---

* And if you don't have any Black friends who aren't just acquaintances, make some!

I was a professional ignorer for a few weeks, until Heather nonchalantly said one afternoon, "Oh hey, Micah and his wife are coming over for dinner. Make sure you're home by five."

What? No! This couldn't be happening. "But, babe . . . why? What do you mean they are coming over for dinner? How did this happen?" My response to her statement was more than over the top, and she just looked at me with that perplexed look on her face and went back to whatever she was doing.*

I spent the afternoon gathering my thoughts. Practicing my arguments. Studying up on the political pundits that I'm sure he was well versed in. Preparing my dissertation defending my points of view. And then they walked in. We small-talked. We small-talked some more. And then I just went for it: "Hey, man. Why did you unfollow me on Instagram?"

Immediately after I asked the question, I felt like an idiot. It was the most junior high moment I'd had in a decade. Thoughts rushed through my mind: *Did I really just ask why he wasn't following me on social media? My dad doesn't even follow me on social media. And besides, Micah never even posts anything. What if he unfollowed everyone? What if he doesn't even check Instagram anymore? Oh my gosh, I just made a complete fool of myself. I can't believe that I just asked him that. I. Am. Taylor. Swift. I may as well just write an entire album about how my feelings get hurt on social media every day. I am no longer a middle-aged man. I am now a K-pop singer with big feelings.*

"Man, because it was making me not like you. And I love you. So I had to stop following you."

---

* I laugh now thinking of my over-the-top response and her being so confused as to why I am the way I am. This is a weekly thought for her, I'm sure: *Why is my husband the way he is?*

[Insert brakes-squealing sound effect.]*

"Huh? What's *that* mean?" I said.

"I've even talked to Melinda [his wife] about this. I don't get it. Suddenly everything you talk about is race. You never used to be like that. I don't know that person that I see on Instagram. Like, I don't even know when you decided to become that person."

At this point, I was beginning to stop listening. I was planning my retort. I began crafting and wordsmithing my response. *Let me teach him what he needs to know,* said the little mental ninja in my mind.

But then he continued: "I seriously don't get it. You aren't even Black." Those words stopped my incredible dissertation preparation. How could I have missed it? How could I have missed it when it was right there in my face? Remember my self-discovery? Remember how I spent most of my life ignoring the Black side of me? Well, guess who I didn't let into that discovery? *The man who was supposedly my best friend.* Sure, we had differing opinions on politics. And yes, my conversations on race were tapping into some political convos here and there. But at the bottom of his frustrations, he was right: He *didn't* know me anymore. And it wasn't his fault.

"You keep calling yourself Black, but your mom is from Mexico and your dad is from Panama, right?"

As he was stating his confusion, I began to lower the volume in my head. The mental ninja put down his throwing stars and went to look for a snack. I allowed my blood pressure to decrease as I prepared him for the same shock I had experienced when I opened that DNA test.

---

* That would be the sound of all my Taylor Swift feelings crashing and burning.

"I get it, Micah. And I want to let you in on something. You love my dad, right?" This was a rhetorical question, because he loved my dad with everything. "And you know what? My dad is Black. Like, just as Black as Shaquille O'Neal and even more Black than Barack Obama. Just because he is from Panama and is Black, all that means is that he's not African American; he's African *Panamanian*." I could see in his eyes as I was explaining that he was having the same aha moment I'd had.

"So my dad is Black. And Panamanian. My mom is White. And Mexican. Their race is Black and White. Their ethnicity is Hispanic." His eyes got even wider.

"This last year, as racial tensions got bigger and heavier, I could no longer ignore the Black part of who I am. It was shoved in my face daily and I couldn't ignore it anymore. For far too long, I chose to ignore it and just lean into my ethnicity as a Latino. But when I go to a fancy store, the security guard follows me because I can't hide what he sees. And when I go fly-fishing and someone writes a note that says 'Go home, $#@$#@%' and leaves it on my truck, I can't hide what he sees. I can't wear a sign around my neck every day, all day, that says 'I'm not Black,' because the truth of it is that I *am*."

• • •

Silence. A good thirty seconds of it. Micah had his hands clasped together, and his thumbs were doing this dance they do when he is thinking hard. "But I don't see you as Black. You're just Carlos. I love you. Just the Carlos guy. Not the Black Carlos. I don't see color when I look at you," he said.

"And that's why I love you," I replied. "Because you love me for *me*. But guess what? I'm about to ask you to do something that I haven't asked you to do before. And I know it's going to be new and weird. I'm going to ask you to love the Black part of me. I need you to *see* that part of me."

He started to cry. I started to cry harder. We stood up and embraced each other and hugged even tighter. It was the most romantic moment in all bromances ever. I love that man, and he loves me. And he'd just had the biggest aha moment of our entire friendship. And so had I. And I knew just how he felt, because I had been there too.

"I promise to do my best, man," he said. "I promise to see you."

Now, I left one important detail out: This entire scene played out in front of all our kids and our spouses. That's right. I need you to go ahead and reread that entire exchange and imagine our kids sitting awkwardly in silence as we got to the heart of our relationship. It was that intense. So we decided something: We decided in that moment not to stand on an issue but instead to walk with people.

How did that play out? We knew we wanted to have some harder conversations about things we didn't necessarily agree on but were passionate about, so we decided to buy season tickets to the brand-new Nashville Major League Soccer team, Nashville SC. That way, we'd be forced to be with each other. Close. Spending good time. Our relationship has since blossomed. I would dare say it's better than it ever was before.

Micah called me a few days after we had our heart-to-heart. "Hey, man. You'll never believe what happened. So, this Black guy came over to my house to work on my plumbing, and he uttered under his breath 'Rich-people problems' to the other plumber. That normally would have pissed me off, but ever since our conversation, I realized something: The plumber's reality is drastically different from mine. And that led to me asking him about his life, and we spent an hour talking about his wife and kids and where he lives. I got to know him in a way I never would have had I not taken the time to truly see him. Look! Our convo is working!"

He was so excited, and that just solidified that this may be the most important takeaway of 2020 for me. Don't stand on issues; walk with people. Here is the truth I want you to know: The only way to walk with someone is to *walk with them*. We gotta get close. We can see so much clearer that way.

Jesus laid this out perfectly when He was the last one walking next to a human whom no one else wanted to get close to. In all four of the Gospels, there is an account of Jesus teaching in the temple when all the super-religious teachers dragged a woman into the center of it. This woman had been caught in the act of adultery. The law of the land said she should be stoned. So there we have it. Open-and-shut case, right? A bunch of old religious guys standing on an issue. Everybody knew where they stood. They stood on the side of punishment. And they were testing Jesus to see what side of the issue *He* stood on. Who would He choose to offend? Who would He make mad? Would He be the law-and-order guy or not? Unfortunately for the people trying to set Him up to fail publicly, Jesus turned the issue human real quick.

> The scribes and the Pharisees brought a woman caught in adultery, making her stand in the center. "Teacher," they said to Him, "this woman was caught in the act of committing adultery. In the law Moses commanded us to stone such women. So, what do You say?" (John 8:3–5)

The issue was clear. They stood on the side of the law of Moses. Now what would Jesus do?

When they persisted in questioning Him, He stood up and said to them, "The one without sin among you should be the first to throw a stone at her."

Then He stooped down again and continued writing on the ground. When they heard this, they left one by one, starting with the older men. Only He was left, with the woman in the center. When Jesus stood up, He said to her, "Woman, where are they? Has no one condemned you?"

"No one, Lord," she answered.

"Neither do I condemn you," said Jesus. "Go, and from now on do not sin anymore." (verses 7–11)

Whoa. Here we have a sinner. Fair enough. Here we also have a group of people looking to punish her who are *also* sinners. In fact, there is only one sinless person in the whole story: Jesus.

And what did He do? He flipped the whole situation around. He made their issue into a person. He then turned the mirror *back on them* so that they could see themselves in the issue. "The one without sin among you should be the first to throw a stone at her" (verse 7). He turned the issue into a human, and then He invited them into her humanity. When that happened, empathy was forced onto the religious people who stood on a certain side of an issue. They could either see themselves in her or stop seeing themselves. And they bounced, one by one.

I know Jesus wouldn't have gloated in that, but *I* would have! ("Bye, Felicia!") That's the humanity in me coming out. But *man,* what a mic-drop moment. Yet this kind of thing was how Jesus did what He did over and over again: He saw humans where others saw issues.

And then look what happened. I love how He continued

and let her know that she was no longer an issue. "Neither do I condemn you" (verse 11).

. . .

There's something to learn there, fam. You know those people in the wrong? On the other side of that issue? The people you can't stand? *Those* people. Jesus's words are for them too. Look at them. See them as people.

"But, Carlos? Those are some bad people!" Sure. Okay. I'm not saying that there aren't consequences for people making bad decisions. But I am saying that to be able to come to any conclusion on an issue, you must walk with the people the issue is touching. Look at them. See them as people.

And even after walking with them, that does not mean that you are going to change your mind. What it does mean is that you will know them in a way that will transform how you look at the issue. Don't stand on issues; walk with people. This right here is what Jesus did all the time. He didn't just let people on a certain side of an issue get away with continually wounding themselves and each other. It's not like His grace on an issue was a free pass from consequences. Rather, it was an opportunity for someone to be seen.

And in turn, their lives changed, whereas if He just viewed them as something to vote against, that progress would never have been made in their lives. Jesus literally told the woman to go and sin no more. She wasn't free to go and continue living recklessly, but she was *free*. And that's the whole point. Jesus walked with her.

You see, *seeing* leads to *freeing*.

SECTION 3

free

free human

Let's say something all together. Out loud. All of us. At the same time. Ready? Well, I guess not really at the same time, because we aren't all reading this at the same time. And maybe not out *loud* if you are reading this while nursing your newborn or if your pet goldfish is napping or something. Or maybe not out loud if you are reading this on your phone in the middle of a meeting. (Hey, pay attention! I'll wait.)

Anyway, if it is safe and at least sort of socially acceptable, let's say something all together. Out loud. All of us. At the same time. Why? Because there is something that happens inside our souls when we declare something out loud. Something that happens when we voice an idea with our own lips into the air, not just in the silence of our thoughts. So, let's do this. You ready?

Wherever you're at, I need you to repeat after me or read this next sentence out loud.

"I can do this."

That's it. That's the sentence.

Because if you're anything like me and you've just read all

these chapters, you may feel as if this human thing is too hard to pull off with such focus. Maybe you think you can just be half-human and half-robot. I don't know. Maybe you think it would be better to just let your life live *you* as opposed to living your life. I mean, *Who has the capacity to honestly be love, be compassion, be justice, be wonder, see bias, see closer, see to serve? Carlos, it's all so much. And, Carlos, can we stop reliving 2020 for a chapter? That alone is triggering me.*

I get it. Really. But I want you to remember something. Something about what I believe about the one we are trying to model this human thing after: Jesus.

Now, remember, there are two types of people who are reading this book: those who believe Jesus is the Son of God and those who don't. And remember I told you that you didn't have to believe in Jesus the Messiah to understand His perfection. You get to look at Him as a historical figure. And if that's the case, you've got it easy. But for those of you looking at Jesus as the picture of perfection, I'm here to tell you that WE CAN'T PULL THIS OFF PERFECTLY LIKE HE DID. But that doesn't mean we don't at least try.

Try to *be* human. Try to *see* human.

And now what? Well, now it's time to put our money where our mouths are. Time to put the action behind the conviction. Time to free humans, and time to be free humans.

• • •

The final section of this book maybe isn't what you initially thought it would be. It's not about just freeing others. I mean, that is going to be the initial push, sure: to use whatever privilege and resources we have to find the humans that could use our help in discovering freedom. But what I have learned from doing this work for a long time is that it's not just those you help free who find the freedom. So many times, *we* find freedom we didn't even know we needed to have. By freeing them, you free yourself. We can't help others be more human without becoming more human ourselves.

I'm not trying to make this sound as corny and self-helpy as it might be coming out, but I promise you it's true. There's brain science (google *mirror neurons* sometime) that says that helping others really does help *us* too. It changes the way we think. The way we see.

We just finished a whole section on how seeing others is really what the world needs to get better at. That is what people so desperately need. But this last step—of freeing them and us—is going to require even closer proximity than just *seeing* them could ever provide.

Do you want to know why people riot? You want to know why people were burning things and looting and doing all sorts of destructive and harmful things in 2020? Sure, there may be many reasons on the surface. But deep down, I think it's because they had been caught in a perpetual cycle of not feeling seen, which leads to not being free. They are imprisoned by their invisibility. Seriously, that's it.

You don't have to do a study on policies and procedure and laws to find out why people were destroying entire streets in 2020 or storming the front doors of the United States Capitol in 2021. It's simple: They feel stuck. They don't feel seen or heard. Now hear me. I'm not saying that looting and rioting is the answer. It's not. But I think we can be confident about the *why*. "We've got to see that a riot is the language of the unheard," Dr. Martin Luther King, Jr., once famously said in an interview. "And what is it that America has failed to hear?" His question still rings out.

• • •

Have you seen the movie *A Christmas Story*? You know, the one with Ralphie.* So, there is this scene in the movie that I think can help us with what I'm trying to explain here.

My favorite scene is when Ralphie wails on that redheaded bully. Remember that scene? Ralphie had been picked on the entire movie, but after years of being bullied, something snapped inside him. Remember the feeling you got when you saw Ralphie beat down the bully? I want you to remember the feeling you got when the beatdown was occurring. Either you were cheering loudly for Ralphie to keep the beatdown going or you felt bad for the bully.

Ralphie didn't premeditate the beatdown. He didn't diagram what corner of the neighborhood he would beat down the bully. He just snapped. You saw it in his eyes.

And, my friend, that is what we saw in summer 2020. It's not a perfect analogy, but the rage part is. Ralphie = Black men being bullied. Bully = racist police and racist systems of oppression. Should Ralphie beat down every bully he meets? No. Did Ralphie's mom shame him? No, she didn't. She understood his pain, and she loved him through his consequences. There were consequences to his actions. There are consequences to ours.

I do not condone rioting. I do not condone looting. I con-

---

* If you haven't, I've got bad news for you: We can't be friends. If you have seen it and can't quote the entire movie back to me, I have bad news for you: We can't be friends. If you have seen it *and* can recite on command every line of the movie, I have good news for you: *We are best friends.*

demn rioting. I condemn looting. I pray it stops whenever I see it happening. But I understand *why* it happens. After years of not being seen, and not being seen leading to not being free, people snap.

So, as humans, how can we help people find freedom before they make devastating decisions that affect themselves and others? We see them and then we free them. Being seen sets people free.

Now, I'm not going to do a deep dive into the socioeconomic policies and ways we can do this collectively as communities. There are way smarter people than I trying to figure that out. But I do want to make this personal. I want to consider what we can do to help people find the freedom they are so desperately looking for. Even if they don't know it, they have a God-given need to be seen. We all want that connection and validation, don't we?

So for this last movement of the book, we want to take our circles of influence, whether large or small, and help those circles heal. And if more and more people help free more and more people, then suddenly we will find ourselves in the middle of a word that has been defined as "an improvement in the condition or strength of something."* That word? *Revival.* A revival of humanity. That's what we all feel needs to happen.

Not a revival of conservative ideas. Not a revival of liberal ideas. Simply a revival of humanity. Humans *being, seeing,* and *freeing.*

And when that happens . . .

Conservative and liberal, pro-vax and anti-vax, abolish-the-police and pro-police, pro-capital punishment and anti-death

---

* *The New Oxford American Dictionary,* s.v. "revival," www.lexico.com/en /definition/revival.

penalty, pro-life and pro-choice, Lakers fans and Warriors fans, LeBron defenders and Jordan defenders—everybody can realize that listening to another point of view doesn't negate your own views. It just helps you see someone else's. And maybe that's just the beginning of a conversation that will lead to freedom for both of you.

Not everything needs to be something you fight for. Not everything needs you to become a culture warrior to defend it at all costs. Not every hill is worth dying on. But can I make one exception to this? I do think that helping course-correct our humanity would be something we would all be better off fighting for in the long run. I think if we can bump us back 1 percent on course, all our political, medical, relational, and sports battles will have a much better chance of seeing some semblance of progress.

There is zero progress without some ability to compromise. We must learn to compromise. But people feel as if that is a four-letter word. Compromise isn't a four-letter word; it's something that we do to get what we think we want. I mean, you do it with your kids for the love. Don't pretend like this is something new and that you aren't willing to do. If you compromise so your three-year-old will eat broccoli, certainly you can compromise with a forty-two-year-old in order to move toward something that you believe in.

Freedom is the entire goal here. What good is it to walk around being compassionate and empathetic if you are still walking around in chains? What good is it if your partner loves who you have become if they are still walking around in chains? If we can't ultimately end up walking without the chains that have bound us for decades, then I'll tell you what: Being human is a waste. And what we will find out in the following chapters is that our humanity is tied to God's divinity.

14

• • •

free loneliness

If you are in chains and do not have the key, you have a few options: You can wait for those who put in you in said chains to show up and take the chains off you, you can try to figure out a way to MacGyver the chains off you, you can give up and die in those chains, or you can wait for a rescuer to come and wrestle the keys away from those who took you captive and then come find you to remove the chains.

Other than the MacGyver option (which, let's be honest, isn't workable for many of us) or the give up and die option, in each of those cases, *someone* has to get near to you to help you get free. They have to breathe the same air that you are breathing in order to take your chains off. They have to go all the way up to you and touch you, to really see and be with you, to notice the way you are locked up, to do what has to be done *closely*. Specifically. There is no way for someone to give you freedom without first touching you.

Herein lies the first facet of freeing humans: the freedom to touch.

• • •

Remember a few chapters back when I was talking about the chariot and Jesus's follower Philip going up to talk to the eunuch? You probably recall that when Philip went to the road, he then went up to the chariot and got *in* the chariot.

And that, my friend, seemed like the most impossible feat imaginable. There were things, social and historical things, that seemed as though they should have kept those two people apart.

But there is one last step. I left it out of the story in order to get us to this point and also because I know that story was already hard enough for many of us to digest while trying to figure out what chariot we were going to have to get uncomfortable enough to walk up to and then freaking climb in. I know that it was a lot. But here we find ourselves many chapters later. Hopefully, you have found the strength to be able to get to the place where you realize that it is less about you being comfortable and more about others being seen.

Here's what happened after Philip got in the Ethiopian eunuch's chariot.

> As they traveled along the road, they came to some water and the eunuch said, "Look, here is water. What can stand in the way of my being baptized?" And he gave orders to stop the chariot. Then both Philip and the eunuch went down into the water and Philip baptized him. (Acts 8:36–38, NIV)

You see, the Eunuch did not find total freedom by simply being seen by Philip. That wasn't the end of the story; that was the beginning of the process of him finding freedom. But what needed to happen was that Philip needed to touch the eunuch. He had to get back out of the chariot and touch him to bring

the eunuch's body in and out of the water they found themselves at so that he could be baptized. This is where the eunuch
finally found freedom—not when Philip saw him but rather
when Philip touched him. And in this story, the touching was
baptism. But that is not the only way.

People are desperate for us to finally get near enough to
free them. At the basic core level, a human needs to be close
enough to touch another human to truly experience everything
that God has for them. And no, I'm not talking about sex or
marriage. You can be single the rest of your life, but I still think
that you need to feel the arms of another human. I still think
that embrace and physical proximity to a community of people
who are for you are vital in your journey toward freedom. We
are social creatures, created to live in community. People need
us near them if they are truly going to be able to find freedom.

· · ·

It was fall 2020. I'd just had a good long honest convo on me
being Black with my best friend. (Remember reading about
that?) The summer had turned to a gorgeous autumn, and
people were replacing their racial rage with their election rage
as we got ready to elect a new president. It's not like one type
of rage really replaced the other, but people found something
new to be angry about, and it was mostly coming from the
pieholes of two men: Joe Biden and Donald Trump.

I, on the other hand, was trying not to have anything to do
with any of that nonsense. I was fully focused on just getting
through the election cycle without too much friend drama. I
was over it. I had already had way more deep convos with
friends than I'd had in the twenty years prior. I'd like to order a
friendship with zero toppings and nothing special, please. I'll

take a little salt and pepper on my friend fries and would like nothing else. Just give it to me plain and simple. That's what I was looking to order from the friendship drive-through at the friendship In-N-Out. No "double double." Nothing "protein style." Nothing fancy. I just needed some regular old friends who argued with me about Jordan versus LeBron, not masks versus no masks. That's it.

And so I decided to invite eight of my closest friends on a fly-fishing trip in Montana. I take this trip every year, but this year, 2020, it seemed especially important for us to get together and drink bourbon, eat good food, fish eight hours a day, and lie about how big of a fish we caught. That's it. I didn't want to talk about anything deep. I. Just. Wanted. To. Fish. And Sleep. And Drink. Can I get a witness? I think at this point in 2020, we were all a bit frazzled from our relationships. It's not that I just wanted to hang with people who thought like me. No, that's not it. I was fine hanging out with people who thought differently than I did. I just didn't want to talk about it.

So off we went. Me and a bunch of friends who were all equally as tired of the chaos as I was. When we got to the lodge, there was this palpable feeling of relief. It was November. We were all so tired of being locked up in our homes and so tired of the noise that was surrounding culture and society. It's okay occasionally to just get away and not think about anything deep. That's what this trip was all about. Nothing deep. Just a bunch of dudes fishing.

At the end of day one, it was exactly what the doctor ordered. We were exhausted from being in the boats all day long slaying fish. Guys were lying about how good of fishermen they were. It was awesome. Jokes and wine were flowing, and we were in heaven.

At the end of day two was more of the same, only this time

we were getting into our feelings a little more. Like our man feelings. Our *meelings,* if you will. (Sorry.)

And then on the morning of day three, my meelings took a turn in a direction that I didn't know was available. "Hey, Carlos, can I talk to you for a second?" Andrew asked.

"Yeah, man. What's up?" I replied, not even remotely thinking that this would be anything other than him telling me that he didn't want to fish that day and he was just going to sit back at the lodge and play his guitar or something.

"So, I don't even know how to tell you this," he said.

"Um, okay. Tell me what?"

"Well, I woke up this morning and didn't feel amazing, but whatever. And then when I went to breakfast, I took a bite of my french toast, and I can't taste anything. Like nothing. And it's not like my nose is stuffed up and I can't taste anything. No, it's like my taste buds aren't working, and I can't smell anything either. What should I do, man?"

You likely remember that my buddy was describing one of the most recognizable signs of Covid. My mind was not prepared for this sort of jolt. But there I sat, the leader of this group, and I had to decide: send him home or wait it out.

Because here's the deal. We had all been living in the same small lodge, eating in the same dining room, sitting in the same hot tub, and laughing at the same jokes for two days straight. He had been in my boat for the entire first day. If he had Covid, well, we all had Covid.

I'm not an epidemiologist, but I was certain that we were screwed. That was the extent of my prognosis.

"Hang tight. Let me check in with the other guys."

So I went over to every guy and let them know one by one. We had one more full day of fishing that day and then we were leaving tomorrow. "Well, Carlos. Come to think of it, I can't taste anything either," another friend said. "I thought that it was weird last night, but I didn't think anything of it."

By the next morning, a few others weren't feeling so well.

• • •

Soon after the event, every single one of us tested positive for Covid. Like, I had straight up hosted a super-spreader event. I was my own worst nightmare. *I used to make fun of people like me,* I thought. *I can't believe I did this.* I was mortified. Not only was I mortified, but by the time I got to a clinic, I also was Covid positive. Perfect score! And I felt like absolute crap.

My sister-in-law and nephews were in town for two weeks, and I wasn't about to be stuck in my bedroom without being able to leave for fourteen days. So I shot out a message to the Instagram masses, and a friend showed up to my driveway with a camper—a Covid camper. If I was going to suffer, I was going to suffer in style.

While I still had energy around day three, I got some string lights and brought out a TV and my PlayStation and some posters and some plants and made the Covid camper my own. Day three was fine. Day six was miserable. Day nine I felt like I was going to die a slow death. Day eleven, I felt better. Day twelve was when it hit me.

I was feeling better. Like, I was back to being able to have a conversation with another human being and it make sense. But I realized something around that point: It was the longest that I had ever gone without touching another human. Ever. Like in my entire life. It was one of the trippiest realizations that I had ever experienced. I had honestly never been that long without human touch. A high five. A handshake. A hug. Nothing. And I started to crave it something fierce.

If I walked onto the deck, my nephews would scream, "Uncle Carlos is on the deck! Run!"

When they would walk past the Covid camper on their way to the car, they would cover their mouths and walk faster. And they weren't doing this to be funny. No, these poor kids were certain that I was some sort of leper. It was horrible. On day fourteen without a fever, I walked to the back door. "Babe? Heather? Can I come inside yet? Can I come back into the fold of the family?" I asked.

"No, babe. Not yet," she answered while mumbling something about the CDC.

I went back to my Covid camper and cried. Not because I was sad that she wasn't letting me back into the house. I cried because I hadn't touched another human being for weeks. Literally weeks. And it was slowly destroying me.

Let me pause here and let everyone know that I realize there are plenty of other people who had it worse than I did. If not touching someone for seventeen days is the extent of what Covid did to me, then I am grateful. I know people who died from Covid. I know people who didn't touch another person for months. My suffering didn't feel like a lot. But at the same time, it did. Right? We only know what we know. And when someone needs a touch, comparing their suffering to someone else's may just be the thing that keeps us from freeing them.

• • •

Everybody around you needs a touch in some way, shape, or form. And it's going to be either our judgment of their level of suffering or others' judgment of us that is going to keep us from getting close enough to touch their stories.

I love that Jesus simply didn't care about either of those things. He was completely unbothered by those who would judge Him and unbothered by a person's level of suffering. I mean, can we just have that word tattooed on our necks? In Old English font: 𝖀𝕹𝕭𝕺𝕿𝕳𝕰𝕽𝕰𝕯.

Okay, maybe that's a bit too far, but I'm really digging this idea of being unbothered on our journey to help others find freedom.

Let's look at one quick story from Jesus's journey.

In Mark 1, His star was rising. In 2022 terms, His Instagram had blown up. *Everybody* was talking about Him. Everybody wanted to see Him. Even the religious leaders were keeping an eye on Him, 'cause He was making some really big claims. He grew up in the synagogues and learned all the Jewish religious laws, and here He was, traveling the countryside, being completely unbothered by these rules while staying bothered by injustice.

> Then a man with a serious skin disease came to Him and, on his knees, begged Him: "If You are willing, you can make me clean."
>
> Moved with compassion, Jesus reached out His hand and touched him. "I am willing," He told him. "Be made clean." Immediately the disease left him, and he was healed. (verses 40–42)

Let's set this up for a second so we can see what was happening here. You see, we have lost the context of a leper in our day and age. This person with this horrendous infectious disease was forced to live alone. Away from other humans. They would be set apart and if they traveled through a town, they were forced by the law to yell at the top of their lungs, "Unclean! Unclean!" because if anyone touched them, they would also be considered unclean and their righteousness would be damaged. You don't get near the lepers, and you don't touch them.

But Jesus.

Jesus was walking from town to town when this leper showed up and got near Him. He begged Jesus to heal him.

Now this is what I want us to get: Jesus did *not* have to touch this leper. According to the Bible, Jesus just spoke things and then they happened. He could heal people a mile away. But what did He do here? Scripture says, "Moved with compassion, Jesus reached out His hand and touched him" (verse 41).

I'm no theologian, but I believe that Jesus was showing those around Him that no religious law was going to get between Him and freeing someone. Now, be careful here. I still do not think that Jesus did it to spite the leaders. It says that Jesus was moved with compassion. Rewind back to chapter 4 to refresh your mind on what compassion is.

Compassion is what moved Jesus to touch the man. And the man was healed. He was free.

My friend, allow the compassion inside you to get you close enough to free someone. You may or may not believe that prayer and laying on of hands can bring healing. I do, but that's not the point here. The point is that you can free someone by simply getting close enough to touch them. Free humans by freely touching their stories. People are all around you. Now go find one and get close.

15

• • •

free life

It's not magic. We don't simply touch someone and then they are free. But touching is essential. Touching gives us the *opportunity* to free them. And, of course, this isn't just physical. It could very well mean you are simply near enough to their story to do something tangible. To allow your action to follow your conviction.

Case in point: You know when you get a text from a friend to do something that you really don't want to do? I mean it could be all sorts of things. Maybe to lend your truck, which inevitably leads to you having to move a large object into said truck. Or for me lately, it's been to help get birds out of friends' attics and homes. I am the first person they call, as if I am somehow now a bird whisperer or Snow White. I put one camera in one bluebird box and suddenly I'm the guy you call when a bird enters your home. Like, my friends fully expect me to walk into their place and whistle, followed by the bird gracefully soaring across the sky of their living room, only to land on my shoulder and then have me walk out. This is the sort of text I don't want to answer. And then there is the sort of text that I don't want to answer asking me to use my platform for something I'm not comfortable with. Like the following text I got a few years back from my friend Shannon.

> Hey friend,
> Any chance you're willing to post about a death-penalty case I'm working on that is scheduled for execution on Thursday? It's from a case I had interned on as a third-year law student twenty years ago. Non-shooter, eighteen just before crime, came at the end of the crime (did not participate in the carjacking) to pick up the co-defendants, and they burned the car down to get rid of fingerprints. Brandon had no idea that the ringleader was going to shoot them, and neither did the other four teens involved. The ringleader was executed in September, two of the other teens are out of prison, and one more (the one I helped represent) is due out in ten years. Brandon was arguably the least involved.

Now, take a moment to process this like I was processing it. I had never in my life talked about the death penalty publicly. And at the time, I didn't really know how I felt about it one way or the other. But what I did know is that plenty of people who follow me had strong feelings to support it. And if there is one thing I know I'm good at, it's getting thousands of people to unfollow me overnight. I know I have that skill down.

• • •

I was so unsure. I walked into the LAX Delta Sky Club and ordered a bourbon neat. I sat next to the north window and just stared at it, thinking for the first time about my opinion about the death penalty. And I kept landing at the same place.

I don't know if I am for or against it. What if he did do it? Shouldn't he die? Is that our decision or God's? Who am I to play God in this man's life? But what about the Old Testament? What about Jesus? Emotions were swirling around in my heart, and they weren't getting easier to navigate the more I worked through them; they were getting more convoluted.

At the end of my thoughts, I was left with this: I trusted Shannon. Like, I *really* trusted her. And if she believed this was something I should do, then I was gonna trust her enough to do it. So I opened up my backpack and pulled out a little phone tripod. (Yes, I travel with a phone tripod. Doesn't everyone?) I found a quiet spot in the sky club and set up my phone on the tripod. I looked at myself in the front-facing camera, took a deep breath, and hit record.

I filled my audience in on what Shannon had sent me. I used all her talking points. I didn't as much try to convince my Instagram family to change their views on the death penalty in general as try to show them the specifics of this case in particular. I gave them an action step: Contact the president and ask him respectfully to save Brandon Bernard's life.

To my surprise, people were jumping on board and sharing my story. Seeing that stories disappear in twenty-four hours and we had only a few days before he would be executed, I made a video that was shareable. I gave actual steps that my people could take in order to help save Brandon's life.

This decision to make a video that will live permanently on my page was a big step. This was akin to the Ahmaud video. There was no turning back once I hit publish, but I had firmly made up my mind: Not only was I going to use my platform to get as close to Brandon's story to help free him myself, but I was going to bring eighty thousand people with me so that they could get close enough to touch him as well.

About fifteen minutes later, my oldest child started screaming.

I jumped up because it was one of those screams where
something is wrong and you know it. "What, babe? What's
wrong?"

"Kim Kardashian just shared your video!"

My lips twisted into a small smile. "I thought something
was wrong!" I replied. She continued to freak out, and I continued to become more emboldened in my plea for people to help
free Brandon.

In the days that passed, Shannon offered me, and in turn
my followers, an inside glimpse like I have never seen before
when it comes to watching an execution play out in real life.
We were petitioning. We were praying. We were trying with
everything we had to help save Brandon.

And then on that final day, the day we were hoping would
not come, we were given access to some words that Brandon
had written (via a Facebook post that has since been removed).

There is no more magical feeling than to feel like the world
is crumbling around you. Your walls are leaning but they
haven't fallen yet. Your foundation is shaky. The roof is
still intact, keeping the rain off you, but it leaks and will
soon go. You want to give up at that point. You want to just
lie down on the muddy ground and let the leaking water
drown you in a puddle. But you can't, because there are
hands that won't let you fall. There is a presence that won't
let you give up.

At that moment, a light starts to shine and the leaks
stop. You walk out with your hands held high and let the
sun warm your cold body. You no longer need the roof; you
are finally free. When you look out, you see an army of

people holding up the wall and patching the leaks. You see that the whole time, you were never alone, and in the front you see the smiling face of Jesus letting you know that He was there the whole time.

I felt like that yesterday. I had done all the sorting of my stuff, and then I was writing my goodbye letters to my family and friends. I felt low and had to stop and take a break. When I felt my lowest, I didn't know that behind the scenes, things were moving. I didn't know that my roof was being repaired while I was looking at the floor to my wet feet.

Even if you don't see it, God is always working for you! Surrender and believe and He will make a way. His will will always be done!

Thank you, God, for giving me the strength to never give up!

When I read that, I got a renewed sense of vigor. You see, when Brandon was at his lowest, even though nobody could physically touch him, we were close enough to his story to touch him. And that touch gave him strength. My friend, I'm telling you that our ability to free humans isn't dependent on our ability to only physically touch them; we just need to get near enough to their story that they *feel* us touching them even if we can't be there in person. You've felt it before. We all have. It's a supernatural thing, really.

. . .

Brandon's story did not end the way we had fought so hard for. Things changed, and not for the better. Politics won out, and despite the best efforts of many people, ultimately the government would put him to death on December 10, 2020. *How could this year get any worse?* I wondered after first hearing the news that he would soon be executed. I'd never fought so hard for a stranger to find freedom. Ever. And there I sat the next morning, weeping into my own hands, wondering if anything we did mattered. And then I got a text from Shannon that answered that question.

> I'm just off the phone with Brandon. He sounded sad but stoic and said he wanted to thank me before this all went down. He said if his life and now death could be used to catalyze change, then that's a worthy cause. We talked about Martin Luther King and the moral arc of the universe. I told him that I hold tremendous gratitude in my heart for him.

"If his life and now death could be used to catalyze change, then that's a worthy cause." I was shook. Ultimately, Brandon didn't get the freedom that we desired, but do you know who did? Me. Something came alive in me. Something unlocked. Something that was quite possibly holding me captive that I never knew was holding me captive. This fight to free Brandon freed me of a caged desire. I began studying the death penalty in America like a law student. The more I researched, the more opposed I became to it. So much so that I've now become a full-fledged death-penalty abolitionist, for more reasons than the word limit on this manuscript will even allow me to unpack. But the point here isn't to get you to become a death-penalty abolitionist; the point is to allow you to realize that when you free someone else, when you get close enough to their story in order to have the ability to unlock their chains with your hands because their hands are unable to, something inside you will find freedom as well. Something inside you will find freedom the more you give freedom. And man, if that's not a sweet deal, I don't know what is.

In this section of the book, it's not hard to find parallels between the greatest human to ever walk the earth and this idea. In Luke, Jesus quoted the prophet Isaiah (see 61:1) when it came to why He was there.

> The Spirit of the Lord is on me,
>> because he has anointed me
>> to proclaim good news to the poor.
> He has sent me to proclaim freedom for the prisoners
>> and recovery of sight for the blind,
> to set the oppressed free. (Luke 4:18, NIV)

If you just read books on Jesus, if you don't even read the Bible, you know that His primary role as He walked those dusty hills of Galilee was to set people free—not only from physical torment, but from mental and spiritual torment as well. He also laid out exactly how we are supposed to pull this off. We talked already about how when Jesus met up with His disciples after He was resurrected, they were like, "Not sure about this resurrected guy." And Scripture says that Jesus *came near*. Well, that passage in Matthew continues to tell us how we are supposed to free humans. We already unpacked this.

> The 11 disciples traveled to Galilee, to the mountain where Jesus had directed them. When they saw Him, they worshiped, but some doubted. Then Jesus came near. (Matthew 28:16–18)

But then after Jesus came near, he continued:

All authority has been given to Me in heaven and on earth. Go, therefore, and make disciples of all nations, baptizing them in the name of the Father and of the Son and of the Holy Spirit, teaching them to observe everything I have commanded you. And remember, I am with you always, to the end of the age. (verses 18–20)

There's that dang word again. The same thing Philip did with the eunuch: *baptizing*. And in order to get that close to someone, you are gonna need to be close enough to touch them.

Freeing humans is going to take touching their hearts and souls, but many times also their person. And oftentimes, our attempts to free humans won't end up with them being free at all. After all, we aren't Jesus. But what may end up ultimately being free is *you*!

Let's think about this principle for a second: The more you free, the more you are free. Is that just feel-good fluff, or is following the way of Jesus in this regard actually going to help us find the freedom we are trying to give?

Let's look at one scientific study in particular.[*] Researchers gathered a group of people and told them that they were going to give them a large sum of money. Half of the group was told to spend that money on themselves; the other half was told to spend their money on someone else. Both groups were told to imagine how they were going to spend it. And so, after the researchers had conducted multiple tests to rule out any other contributing factors and after MRI brain scans were performed

---

[*] Elizabeth W. Dunn, Lara B. Aknin, and Michael I. Norton, "Prosocial Spending and Happiness: Using Money to Benefit Others Pays Off," *Current Directions in Psychological Science*, 23, 41–47, April 1, 2014, https://journals .sagepub.com/doi/10.1177/0963721413512503.

on the participants, the data was overwhelmingly clear: The group of participants who were told that they were going to give the money away were happier. Regardless of the participant. Regardless of the amount of money. Just the thought of being generous was enough.

Science is out there proving what Jesus was showing us: that freeing people frees us. And the incredible thing is that it doesn't take abolishing the death penalty (though I'd love to do that) to free someone. The goal is for you to walk around your days realizing that by freeing people around you, you will find freedom as well. Simple freedom. A win-win. Like paying for the people's coffee in the car behind you in the drive-through. Like sticking twenty bucks under a stranger's car-door handle. Like complimenting someone on their smile. Like after asking someone how their day is and when they give you the classic "Good," asking them sincerely, "What does 'good' mean?"

People find freedom when we see them. And when that happens, we will begin to find some of that freedom as well.

16

. . .

free me

We did it! The Whittaker familia made it through 2020!
By the skin of our teeth, but still. The year 2020 tried
to take us out over and repeatedly.* I'm serious. On Christmas
morning 2020, my family and I were opening presents when
we *felt* a loud boom. Notice I didn't say *heard*, because the
sound we heard was much softer than what we felt. The windows shook for a second, and Heather and I looked at each
other like, *Are we at war? Is 2020 gonna end with World War III?*
We live approximately three miles south of downtown Nashville, and I did what any Gen X dad would do: I opened up
Twitter. Within thirty seconds, #NashvilleBombing was trend-
ing. Someone had loaded an RV with explosives and blown up
an entire city block on Second Street. I was in shock. Our
Christmas continued throughout the day with all of us checking in on what was happening downtown, grateful for our
safety. There is nothing more jarring than an explosive attack
in your own city *on Christmas morning* to remind you of the

* By the way, if you're someone who lost loved ones that year or otherwise
just *didn't* really make it, I want you to know I see you. God sees you too.

real meaning of Christmas. That was the cherry on top of 2020. Thanks, but no thanks. *Dear Universe, please send us 2021, ASAP.*

My family and I found ourselves on a Delta flight to Sacramento on January 6. We were getting the heck out of Nashville for a few days of skiing in Lake Tahoe. I was going to be off social media and do nothing but ski and sip black coffee. Also, I was going to keep a close eye on the boyfriends (as suddenly there are boyfriends allowed on our family vacation—*what is happening?*).*

I was already feeling the stress of the real world leaving my shoulders. As we flew over the Sierra Nevadas, I could almost smell the pine trees and cold air mingling together with some "cheap" hot dogs the ski resort was selling. I had not even logged on to Wi-Fi on the flight because I didn't want to see what was happening in the world. The pilot got on the intercom: "Ladies and gentlemen, we are starting our initial decent. We should be landing shortly in Sacramento."

After the wheels hit the ground, I turned on my phone and it started buzzing. But buzzing more than normal. Like nonstop notifications from Twitter and iMessage. Normally, the buzzing would have freaked me, as I'd be thinking that something had happened to one of my kids or my wife and they were trying to get a hold of me. But they were all here (along with their boyfriends—ugh). I turned on my phone and saw a message from my friend Nick: "Bro, the Capitol is under attack. The U.S. Capitol. Are you watching this?"

---

* Free advice to parents: Take the new boyfriends on vacation so they are locked in a small condo with you if you wanna find out what they are really like. ☺

Immediately, Christmas morning came rushing back into my head. The feeling of *Oh my gosh, it's World War III*. That was the same thought I had, only this time I wasn't imagining it. Some nation was attacking our nation's Capitol building. I didn't know who invaded our borders, but I do remember that I felt the same way I felt on 9/11. I didn't want to freak Heather out, but I immediately began taking inventory of our agenda and how we were going to get home if California was somehow under attack as well. We were landing in the state capital, after all. It made sense that whoever invaded our borders could target Sacramento. These were the thoughts running through my head after I read that text from Nick and before I opened Twitter. Imagine my complete shock and horror when I realized after looking at Twitter for less than two seconds that our legislators were not running from an attack by a foreign country. No, our elected representatives were under attack *from Americans*.

I won't bore you with the details of that day. I'm sure you watched it unfold too. We all watched in horror. People on the left and people on the right. This wasn't a partisan shock. Other than the most extreme conservatives, *everyone* was shocked at what was unfolding in real time before our very eyes. By the time we got to the hotel, there was a *Braveheart*-looking shirtless man, complete with horns on his head, waving a flag from the speaker of the house's chair in the U.S. Capitol. "These people are insane," I said to Heather. "What is happening?"

And then I saw them. I saw a photo of a rope and a noose on the lawn of the Capitol building. I saw a photo of a man marching around the Capitol carrying a flagpole with a Confederate flag hanging from it.

. . .

What was I seeing? What in the world was happening? I didn't have to make a single post on Instagram for my people to know what I was feeling. I didn't have to text a single friend for them to know the boiling that my blood was doing. But the truth is that the whole thing made me less angry and more sad. A heart blanket of "It's useless. There's nothing I can do to help people become more human" fell over me. I was in absolute shock. That image of the man with the flag in my nation's Capitol haunted me.

So as I often do, I found a few words to simply describe what I was feeling. What I wrote on Instagram wasn't a summation of all truth, but it was what I was feeling in that moment.

My words aren't going to be poetic this time.

I've been willing to engage in thoughtful conversation for four years while trying to not offend those I love who loved this president.

I've tried with my words to explain how his rhetoric enables and encourages those who don't like people that look like me.

I've tried with words.

Now I'm just grateful I've found a picture.

A picture from today.

This picture is the summation of everything I've been trying unsuccessfully to say.

Make America Great Again?

Nah.

This guy and his flag walking the halls of the Capitol in

support of that phrase is why when we see MAGA hats and hear "Make America Great Again," people who look like me get physically nauseous.

I love my country.

I love her dearly.

And I've got news for this guy and his people:

I'm not gonna let you take us *back* to your version of "great again."

♥♥♥

This was a very raw post. It was what I felt in that moment. It was a very *biased* post. I know it was. I knew it was when I wrote it. But I felt like I needed to share it. Why? Because although it was filled with my personal bias, it let people into a small window as to why many Blacks felt the way they felt about that phrase.

I have really good friends who don MAGA hats and apparel, and to them, it doesn't even remotely mean what it means to the man holding that flag in the photo. So I know that they would never attack the Capitol and parade around rubbing history in my face to wound me so deeply. I know this. But I also know what I know: that this day was a culmination of people desiring to take us back to their version of "great." And I wasn't having it. I know it's the Black Lives Matter thing. That phrase does not mean the same thing to every person who says it or wears it. We must be nuanced in our conversations. From both sides. But that doesn't mean emotion isn't elicited by the mere sight of something that shakes you to your core.

I hit Post and then waited for the thunderous pushback.

There really wasn't any. At least not from people who followed me. I'd say that my audience sits fifty-fifty on both sides of the aisle. This isn't a political thing; this is a human thing. Everything I had been saying to my friends about how words can spark hate was unfolding right before our eyes. It disturbed us all.

That day ruined a lot for me. It decimated much of the hope I had that we could right the ship. It took me from "We've got this" to "They got us." I was gutted. I felt more shackled than I care to admit. It was written all over my face. "Hey, babe, you can't let this ruin our vacation," Heather said. "I know it weighs heavy on you, but we took this trip so we could bond and heal a little. Remember?" She was right. But how could I find any sort of solace while skiing on a mountain in a country where the Capitol could be taken over by a bunch of stick-yielding terrorists? It was so unsettling.

I did my best to have a good few days. I skied. I read. I coffee-d. And I cried. (Shocker, I know.) Why did I cry? Because I was given freedom from another human when I didn't even know I needed it.

· · ·

This free-human thing—it really works. You see, I've got this friend. His name is Rob. He is one of my closest friends. We laugh more together than I do with many friends. I call Rob my middle-aged White conservative friend. Ha! I know that probably describes most of my friends, but it's become a joke between him and me. And here's the thing: For some reason, Rob and I have stayed really close over the past few years of friend trauma I'd been through because of the growing distance in ideals with many of my guy friends. But with Rob, it was different. It's not like we didn't talk about the issues. It's not like we didn't talk about the hard stuff. We did. It's just that we didn't let that get in the way of our relationship. We were both doing the whole "Don't stand on issues; walk with people" thing. I didn't reach out to him during what was unfolding. I didn't really reach out to anyone.

Heather and the kids were inside a grocery store when I got a text while waiting in the car for them to come out. The text was from Rob. All he wrote were three words: "I see now."

And that was all it took for the floodgates to open up, and I began to cry. Like, ugly-cry. It's kind of as if I had been holding my breath and I didn't know I was. Like I was breathing with only 20 percent of my lungs and was clueless until I finally got a real breath. Like I was carrying something on my shoulders that I didn't know was there and then suddenly it wasn't. It was one of those moments. And so I ugly-cried.

I texted Rob back. "Seriously. You are my hero for continuing to try and see."

Three words from a super-close friend who lives on the opposite side of the aisle than I do.

Three words that finally broke me and I wept.

My middle-aged White conservative Trump-voting friend, whom I love dearly.

We have had many deep talks over the past four years: me explaining the depths of my concern, and him listening and explaining his. The goal wasn't to turn him from his conservative roots. The goal wasn't to make him lean left. It was simply to be seen. And I've felt seen.

But that day, after an exhausting twenty-four hours, to see a notification from this dear friend who I would catch a bullet for, and it simply said, "I see now." That didn't mean he was turning his back on his values; it simply meant he was facing me and protecting mine.

And that, my friend, is a picture-perfect example of what it looks like to *free* someone. To free a human. Because so many times, those who need freedom don't even know it. They don't know that they are carrying the weight of the world until you show up and take it off them. That's why this part is so crucial. You can't just look for humans who are screaming out in agony that they need help. Of course there will be humans we can free who are blatantly in need of freedom. But I bet you Rob didn't know that his three little words would give his middle-aged Black a-little-more-liberal friend the freedom that he didn't know he needed. The relief that he didn't know he wanted.

Rob didn't turn into a Democrat; he simply saw deeper into my story and let me know. Three words unlocked something in me that needed unlocking. So, the question now is, Who can you send three words to that could breathe breath back into their lungs after years of them holding their breath without even knowing?

Free humans. *Free* can turn from a verb to an adjective in three seconds flat.

What if I told you that you can't truly understand how to fully free someone unless you are free yourself? What if I told you that you may be able to accidentally free someone but you won't be able to truly get into this final step of freeing humans unless you are truly free yourself? I wrote a book a few years back that helps you with all that. It's called *Kill the Spider,* and it's an essential read if you are stuck on this part, but you might be closer to freedom than you think you are. Just knowing that may be enough to push you toward the final few chapters in this book. Your freedom is near!

So why don't you text someone who you haven't been able to see eye to eye with in a while and find something that you now see clearly from their point of view? The breath that escapes their lungs from reading your words may be strong enough to blow you off your feet.

Hang tight, 'cause the next few chapters are going to increase those breaths all around you to where you are standing in the middle of a free-human hurricane.

Here we go.

17

• • •

free indeed

There we were, mouths hanging open. All of us. In shock at what we all saw. There wasn't a single conservative friend of mine that was defending what happened on January 6. Not a single one. That is when I knew for certain that the television media had it in for us, because everyone on the news networks was trying to convince America that most conservatives loved January 6 or that the insurrectionists were liberal actors.

It was a mess. *Just turn the TV off, Carlos,* I thought. *It's not real.* (Put that on a T-shirt stat: *Just Turn Off The TV, Carlos.*) We were tired.

And so began 2021, with an insurrection and then all of us realizing that maybe all this hate had gone too far. I felt like there was a palpable shift in so many people. So many I ran across were seriously exhausted of hating each other. It's not necessarily what the news wanted us to hear; they wanted us to hear that we were growing even more and more divided. But my unscientific study of those I was sitting next to on trains, planes, and automobiles was telling me different. People were so tired of hating people they had loved for so long. People were ready to get back in relationship with their great-aunt Hilda who was sending them conspiracy theories every other day. People were ready to get back into relationship with their best friend Chris who was convinced that every single White person was a deep-seated racist. I think even great-aunt Hilda and best friend Chris were exhausted from their own conspiracies, right?

I began to see even the most intense of heated relationships soften. Why? Because we were not created for such high levels of intense relationship 24/7. That can't be maintained. And after a year of it, people were coming back around. I even remember seeing some familiar names and faces that I had not seen in almost a year on my Instagram feed again. As March approached, I posted some thoughts on the Ahmaud Arbery shooting that had happened a year prior. I saw a few people reposting my video, people who had not only left the year before but had left in a huff and let me know about it.

People would DM me telling me that they were leaving or unfollowing me. I never understood that. Like, when I unfollow someone, I simply just hit unfollow. I don't DM them to let them know I am unfollowing them. When did that become a thing? And to be completely honest, 73 percent of those who would DM me to let me know that they were unfollowing me I would just ignore. But the other 27—I would always thank them for letting me know that they were unfollowing me but then would also remind them that I am not an airport. This is not Carlos Whittaker International Airport, so there was no need to announce their departure.

I told you I'm not the human you need to be learning how to human from. That's Jesus. That ain't me. ☺ But I *was* sincerely overjoyed to see so many members of my former Instagram fam coming back. It was like we all were taking stock of the relationships we were missing and coming back to see who was safe enough to hang out with again. I know that social media is normally a one-way relationship, which isn't a relationship at all, but I will tell you that I try my hardest to treat everyone as though we are friends. I mean, some of you talk about me to your other friends as if we are friends, and we have never met before! That's the goal. I wanna be that Insta-fam you never had.

. . .

Let's roll ourselves toward March 2021. I felt as though humanity was at least attempting to heal, if only a small fraction.

But can I get as real as I have been in a hot minute? I was tired, yo. I was tired from a year of educating people who did not want to be educated. I was tired from a year of forgiving those who didn't care if they were forgiven. I was tired. I was exhausted. I knew deep in my heart there was hope for humanity, but man was it hard to see. Especially after January. I didn't know if I could maintain the energy that it took to continue the good fight. I was ready to take my account back to being nothing more than my filming the robins in my front yard, along with maybe the occasional joke poking fun at Whataburger and causing massive division between myself and the entire states of Texas and Oklahoma. Like *that* was the content I was ready to get back to. We'd had a bad year. *Lord, can I just take an Instagram content-creator union break?*

And it wasn't just me. Seeing that my little family desperately needed a break as much as I did, we decided to tack on a family trip to a work trip I was taking at the end of March. I was going to be speaking at a church in Denver, so we planned a few days to head to Breckenridge to ski. Heather is a master snowboarder, and I still ski with my seventh-grade ski bib on, but whatever. We all love the snow, so the tickets were bought. I thought that this was exactly the freedom we needed. Just run away and act like nothing was wrong. (I am a fan of this. It's called vacation, and we all deserve one.) No shame in our game when it comes to pretending things are better than they are. About a week before we were supposed to go to Denver, we woke up to a frantic call from my oldest daughter, Sohaila, around 6:30 A.M. "Dad, I've been in a wreck. I was on my way to work and a car swiped my side." My heart started pounding.

"I'm okay," she said, "but I need you."

That is exactly the sort of phone call that you dread getting as a parent. But at least she wasn't injured. That was five days before we were supposed to leave. A totaled car. But a safe daughter. The next night, Nashville got hit with a massive storm. We are used to storms here in Nashville, but this wasn't a storm with lots of wind and tornado concerns. This was simply tons and tons of rain. It rained, like, nonstop *hard* rain. All night. All the next day. And the next night too. And then my daughter and her boyfriend went to the basement to watch a movie (bad idea, dads), and when she got to the bottom of our carpeted stairs, she yelled "Daaaaaad!"

We hadn't been in the basement all day long, and when I rounded the corner from the kitchen to head down the stairs, I still didn't know what was wrong. "Look, Dad," she said. "Look at the carpet. It's moving."

I walked a few more steps down and then she stepped on the carpet. It moved like the sheet on top of my aunt Nancy's waterbed back in the seventies. I ran past her and took a nervous step onto the carpet. Water came rushing up through the rug and onto the side of my sneaker. "Kids!" I yelled, "Hurry! We've got to get this furniture upstairs now!" Everyone went and grabbed their rain boots, and we began rapidly moving furniture. We emptied all the bottom cabinets holding the photo books and old VHS tapes that we had collected. We opened the door to the driveway and started sweeping as much water out as we could. But it was no use. More and more water was coming into the basement from under the cabinets. I went into the house's storm shelter and found the root of the problem: Water was rushing in from the corner of the shelter. There was no way we were stopping it. Our best bet was to just let nature take its course and get as much out as we could.

By midnight, the water was up to the middle of my shin. Our basement and garage were completely flooded, and all our basement furniture was now upstairs piled with fans pointed at it all. It looked like a war zone. *Ugh. Please just get us to Thursday and onto that plane to Denver.*

When we woke up the next morning, three days till Denver, Heather and I looked at each other and laughed. It was that sort of "Can you believe that happened?" laugh. Deep breath. Just a few more days till vacation. Then? "Babe, Pope isn't eating anything," I heard later that morning.

Pope is our beautiful Bernese mountain dog of eight years. He has a sensitive stomach and had obviously got into something. He's a trouper. So we just kept an eye on him all day. Around 6 P.M., he still wasn't really moving, so Heather decided to take him to the vet. We just locked eyes and shook our heads. No laughs were coming out at this point. *How much is that vet bill gonna cost?* Heather called me from the vet. "He's got a stomach bug. They said he will be fine, but it cost us five hundred dollars." Great. My dog got to enjoy a snack that ended up causing his stomach to swell and my wallet to shrink. And our house looked as though we were blocking all the doors with sofas in case the zombie apocalypse ended up happening.

I looked at Pope when he got home and hoped he could feel me thinking how much trouble he was in for eating whatever he ate. *Almost to Colorado,* I thought. *We can do this.*

The next day, Pope had a little more of his zip back. *Phew. That was close.* I was on a Zoom interview for a podcast. I was the guest on the podcast and I was mid interview with this super-kind woman who was deeply into the next question that she was asking me when Heather FaceTimed me. Only she was in the garden 'cause she didn't want to be in the house while I was on this interview.

Maybe she just forgot. I hit Decline. But then she called again.

You know that sixth sense you get when you just know something is wrong but you ignore it? And of course I ignored it. BECAUSE HOW COULD ANYTHING BE WRONG WHEN SO MUCH WRONG HAD ALREADY HAPPENED?

The third time she called, I apologized to the woman doing the interview and answered the FaceTime. "You need to come out here," Heather said. She was weeping. "All my chickens are dead."

Now, I need to pause here to let you know how much my wife loved her chickens. They all had names. We had them for a few years. They followed her around and were actually more intelligent than my dog. (Pope, if you ever read this, I'm sorry, and obviously I was wrong, and also *how have you been hiding the fact that you can read?*)

"Please come now. An owl killed them, killed them all."

I hung up the phone, and the poor lady interviewing me was just staring at me on the Zoom call with her mouth hanging open. She had been reading about our horrible week on Instagram, so she knew this was crazy. "Just go help your wife. We can finish this later," she said.

I slammed the laptop shut and ran outside. On the way out, I was less concerned about the chickens and more intrigued by how my wife knew that it was an owl that had killed them. Like, how did she know? As I approached the chicken coop and Heather, she was crying and pointing. I looked where she was pointing and saw Mary, her favorite chicken. I went up to Heather and wrapped my arms around her. "Baby, I'm so sorry."

"No, Carlos. Look again!" she yelled.

And as I cocked my head right, I saw a really big chicken tangled up in a sort of netting, only on second glance, I realized that it wasn't a chicken at all. Right there about ten feet in front of me was the murderer of all six chickens. Right there in front of me was a *massive* great horned owl. Tangled up but alive. "Baby, that's an owl!" I yelled.

The next hour of our day was spent untangling this huge owl while trying not to injure it any further. After we got enough string from around its wing, it tried to fly away, but its wing was injured. My Snow White of a wife somehow chased this huge owl. I don't think you, my dear friend, realize how large this thing was, so let's just call it a triceratops. She chased the triceratops, somehow captured it in a towel, and slowly made her way back to me. The triceratops gazed lovingly into her eyes. (Go watch the "worst week" highlight on my Instagram to see how massive this thing was.)

We drove it to an animal-rescue center about an hour outside Nashville and made it home before dinner. *Two days till Colorado. Jesus take the wheel.*

The next day, we were all a little shook. If *you* aren't shook by now, I need you to reread this chapter. What in the world was happening? We had to just get through the remainder of this day, and tomorrow at 6 A.M. we would be on a plane to

Colorado. The day was fine. But then that night while we were packing, Pope went outside and buried himself under a bush. He was shaking. We tried to bring him back inside, but he weighed over a hundred pounds. He had been doing okay for a few days, but something was definitely wrong.

"Babe, we gotta take him to the vet again," Heather said. "We can't leave him like this with the dog sitter."

We dropped him off at the vet. Around 8 p.m., I got the call. We were all still packing, but you could feel the tension in the house. Nobody wanted to leave while Pope was this sick.

"Mr. Whittaker," the vet said, "I have some bad news. His kidneys are failing, which led to his liver being damaged and his heart . . ." and on and on she went until I didn't really need to hear anymore but still kept listening, trying to keep it together. I was pacing out on the back deck, with my family waiting on pins and needles inside for an update. The vet told me how much it would cost to try to see what else was wrong, to possibly buy him a few more weeks, but I already knew what I didn't want to know. What none of us wanted to know.

When I walked inside, I didn't need to say anything. Everyone knew. We all immediately started bawling. "Can we go see him?" Sohaila asked. "Yeah, baby," I replied. "Let's go say goodbye."

I lay on the cold floor of the room with my best friend. We stayed face-to-face until he left this earth for somewhere far greater. I was the last one in there with him. After it all, I walked to the car and yelled at the top of my lungs, "GOD, WHAT IS HAPPENING? WHY ARE YOU DOING THIS TO US?" I was so confused.

I got home, got on Instagram, and posted an incredible photo of Pope and eight words: "Words may fail me, but you never did."

And with that, I called a family meeting. "We can't still be going to Colorado in the morning. It's midnight. We take off in six—"

Heather interrupted, "Why would we stay here and be sad in our flooded house with no Pope and no chickens?" She was right. We packed our bags and loaded them into the car.

"Okay, kids. Go to sleep. Be up at 4 A.M. We're gonna get outta here."

I could hear each kid individually crying themselves to sleep, and soon I did as well. This had been the hardest week we'd ever had.

• • •

As a human, I was confused, I was defeated, and I was exhausted. Also, I was in desperate need of freedom. But how in the world was someone supposed to free me? How were we supposed to be free of the collective trauma we were going through? I know that our week was rough, but I was having a hard time not comparing our suffering to the suffering of others. Remember, we talked about this a few chapters back. I wasn't allowed to compare my suffering and lessen what I was feeling. But it was hard. At the same time, I knew that my family needed a win. We were at the edge of our emotions. We needed to be free from whatever hell was happening to us. And I didn't know where that freedom would come from, not to mention how much more we would need only a few hours later.

Yes, things were really bad. But somehow they were about to get worse.

18

. . .

free extravagantly

"There's no way this is true."

"I never thought Carlos was a liar."

"I was with this guy until this point in the book, but this is a bit much, man."

I'm giving you people all the credit, because had I been holding this book in my hands as I read the previous chapter, I don't know if I would even turn the page to get to the next one.

But all those things happened. I could write fifty thousand words about *just that week*. The insanity that was in the details of that week is too much for this book. I don't think even Steven Spielberg would write a script with that much drama.

As we were stumbling into the security-screening line the next morning at 5 A.M., I don't think any of us could believe everything that had happened either. Except for the fact that Heather was sobbing in line. She sobbed all the way to the plane. She sobbed as we took off from Nashville toward Atlanta, where our layover was. She sobbed as we landed in Atlanta. She sobbed as we got off the plane. And when I say sobbed, I mean it. No exaggeration.

As I looked around at the kids, I could see that they were all suffering in their own unique ways. Losiah and Seanna were stoic. Sohaila and Heather were crying. I was just trying to make sure everyone was okay and that we'd get to the next flight on time. We were seven hours removed from putting our family dog to sleep. *Just. Get. Us. To. Denver.*

We headed down the terminal toward the escalators. If you have ever been to the Atlanta airport, you know the escalators I'm talking about. There are three escalators, parallel to one another and at least five stories tall, that look like they are going to and from heaven.

When we approached our down escalator, Heather and Sohaila were about twenty feet in front of Losiah, Seanna, and me. They got on the closest escalator to the wall. We got onto the center escalator and they were about twenty feet below us when Losiah got on behind me. They were nearing the bottom of the escalator when a man got on their escalator. I looked up at him for some reason. I don't know why. He was about thirty years old and was looking at his phone while holding his hard-shelled suitcase in his other hand. And then I saw it happen.

For some reason, he lost his grip on his suitcase. His eyes got big and mine got bigger. He lunged for it but missed, and I heard the sound. Like a bobsled at the Winter Olympics, his suitcase started sliding down the Terminal A escalator, straight at my wife and daughter. They were at the very bottom. The suitcase was coming from the top with nobody and nothing between to cushion the missile. It was like slow motion and fast motion mixed in one. I barely had time to get the first syllable of Heather's name out before the rocket of a heavy suitcase closed in on her. She heard it at the last second and with her mother's instinct pushed Sohaila out of the way. And then I saw my wife's legs go into the air and her torso onto the escalator stairs.

"Babe!" I yelled. The three of us began running and pushing past all the people on our way down to her. When we got to the bottom, she was sobbing in a way I don't think I had ever seen her sob before. This was deeper. It was almost a spiritual mourning. Everyone was panicking. "Are you okay? Babe, are you okay?" I asked. Sohaila was on the phone with our friend Wes to start praying.

"It's broken," Heather said. "My wrist is broken." I didn't even know what to say. The poor guy who took out my wife was wondering why we were *all* weeping and gnashing our teeth. "Man, you wouldn't even understand. Go ahead and catch your flight. I know you didn't mean to do it. Just go ahead. We will be okay." (Look at what happens when my Enneagram 9 takes over.) By now, a few security guards had shown up and Heather's wrist was swelling badly.

I need you to understand something: I honestly thought I was dreaming at this point. You know when people in the movies slap themselves because they want to wake up from a bad dream? I did that. I slapped myself, secretly hoping that I would wake up to my non-flooded house with our family dog, Pope, licking my face.

But it didn't work like in the movies. (If this is a dream, I am still in it.) If anything, I think the paramedics who showed up were about to put me on a stretcher as well because I was so upset.

• • •

We called some friends who lived in Atlanta to pick up the kids. I followed the paramedics with my wife in a wheelchair to wherever it is they keep the ambulances at the Atlanta airport. Heather was in massive pain. We got in the ambulance and the paramedics drove us *on the tarmac in between planes* to the airport exit. We arrived at Grady Memorial Hospital, and by this point Heather had gotten some pain meds and was feeling a bit better.

With Covid protocols, I couldn't go in with her. And that was how I found myself standing outside the hospital in downtown Atlanta with two suitcases in the rain and nowhere to go. I did the only thing I knew to do at that moment: I dialed my pastor. She answered on the first ring.

"Hey, Carlos. Are you guys okay? I heard the bad news," Alex said.

I was grateful someone had gotten a hold of her before I did. "I don't know, Alex. Like, I can't believe all this is happening to us. I'm freaking out a little bit."

"Well just enjoy the snow, okay? You guys deserve a few days off. Have you landed yet?" she asked. It was then that I realized she had no idea why I was calling. She thought I was calling to be consoled about our dog dying the night before. BECAUSE OF COURSE THAT WOULD HAVE BEEN THE WORST THING THAT COULD HAVE HAPPENED TO US IN THE TWELVE HOURS SINCE IT HAPPENED.

"Oh no. Alex, do you not know what has happened since then?" I said.

"What? No. Where are you?"

"I'm standing outside Grady Memorial Hospital in Atlanta. Someone dropped a suitcase down the escalator at the airport, taking Heather out. She broke her wrist." I didn't even believe what I was saying, because who could?

"Carlos, oh no."

"Alex? I have a question. And I need the real pastor answer because I didn't go to Bible college or anything like that. So shoot straight with me. Are we cursed? Is *that* what is happening? Does someone have a voodoo doll of me and they're poking needles in it? What is happening?"

"Oh, Carlos. You aren't cursed, love," Alex replied. "You are just having a really crappy week. You know, sometimes we just have crappy weeks. You aren't cursed."

And I have no idea why that made me cry in relief. But it did. It all came out. I cried like I needed to cry all week. I cried harder than I did the night before when Pope passed away. I cried harder than I had cried in a long time. We weren't cursed; we were just having a really crappy week.

That gave me the energy to march back into the hospital and sneak my way into the section of the hospital Heather was at. We were gonna be okay—I could feel it.

My phone buzzed. I looked down and saw over a hundred unread messages. Usually, this is normal for me, but that would be *all* my unread messages. These were from the last *hour*. I then realized that I had asked people to pray on Instagram, leaving them hanging after the suitcase had smashed my wife. The last message was from my friend Sharon.

"Hey, friend. Are you guys okay? Could you do something for me? Could you give me your Venmo?" she asked.

Now, listen, I'm a lot of things. Proud is not one of them. But I also knew that I was not about to give her my Venmo. I can pay my own bills. There are plenty of people in worse spots than I was. *Much* worse. I didn't need charity. Prayers and well wishes were enough. "I'm not giving you my Venmo, Sharon," I replied.

"You either give it to me or I'm going to find it," she said. "Your choice."

Now, you need to know that Sharon isn't your average "Give me your Venmo" friend. She had *lots* of followers. I knew what was about to happen if I gave her my Venmo. I was preparing for all the "I don't deserve this" speeches I was going to have to give, and I just felt that God told me to stop comparing my suffering and to just receive. I had given and given for twelve months, and it was my turn to receive.

I gave her my Venmo. Within seconds, my phone started buzzing nonstop. My push notification sound for Venmo was not on silent, so it started making that cash-register-from-the-eighties sound effect. And it kept making that sound over and over for hours. It wasn't about the money; it was about the love. It was about knowing—*knowing*—that we weren't in this by ourselves.

· · ·

Before I finish this story, I need us to realign with Jesus again. What I was feeling in that moment was the same thing that this newlywed husband was probably feeling when he ran into Jesus for the first time.

On the third day a wedding took place at Cana in Galilee. Jesus' mother was there, and Jesus and his disciples had also been invited to the wedding. When the wine was gone, Jesus' mother said to him, "They have no more wine."

"Woman, why do you involve me?" Jesus replied. "My hour has not yet come."

His mother said to the servants, "Do whatever he tells you."

Nearby stood six stone water jars, the kind used by the Jews for ceremonial washing, each holding from twenty to thirty gallons.

Jesus said to the servants, "Fill the jars with water"; so they filled them to the brim.

Then he told them, "Now draw some out and take it to the master of the banquet."

They did so, and the master of the banquet tasted the water that had been turned into wine. He did not realize where it had come from, though the servants who had drawn the water knew. Then he called the bridegroom aside and said, "Everyone brings out the choice wine first and then the cheaper wine after the guests have had too much to drink; but you have saved the best till now."*

What Jesus did here in Cana of Galilee was the first of the signs through which he revealed his glory; and his disciples believed in him. (John 2:1–11, NIV)

You've likely heard this story of Jesus's first miracle before. I mean, if you've spent any time around church, how could you not? But I want us to look at the absurdity of this moment. The absurdity of the generosity that Jesus showed everyone at that wedding in that moment. You see, when the story begins, it seems that the wedding had been going on for quite some time. How do we know that? Because it says that Mary went to Jesus and said that they had run out of wine. Now, I am no maître d', but I did know that you don't run out of wine at the *beginning* of a wedding; you run out of wine at the *end* of a wedding. So, this generosity was about to happen at the end of the wedding. The groom was probably embarrassed. I mean, if I put myself in his sandals, I would be embarrassed. Right? You run out of the good stuff? But never fear—the water-into-wine master is here.

When Mary asked Jesus to do it, He kind of lips off to her.

---

* At least as long as I've been in church, Baptists have been saying that He turned water into grape juice. LOL!

Look! He does! "Woman, why do you involve me?" (verse 4, NIV). He seems a bit put off, but it's His mom. And, of course, He does what she asks even after a little bit of attitude. Nobody ever said Jesus never had attitude. And I love how Mary takes His words and turns to the servants and, like what I would imagine an Italian mother saying, she says, "Do whatever he tells you" (verse 5, NIV). (I hope you read that with an Italian accent.) So, it says that Jesus asked them to fill the thirty water jugs—*thirty!*—with water. And it says that "they filled them *to the brim*" (verse 7, NIV, emphasis added). This is an important detail. So let's do the math.

There were 6 jars of 30 gallons each. That equals 180 gallons, which would be 682 liters, which would be the equivalent of 908 bottles of wine.

Nine hundred and eight bottles of wine.

That seems preposterous. Who *does* that? Who gives above and beyond what anyone is expecting? No way they can drink that. And this isn't like giving a 25 percent tip to the waitress; this is like giving the waitress a winning lottery ticket. This generosity He displays is insane. And before you say it was grape juice, I need you to reread the main master of ceremonies' words: "Everyone brings out the choice wine first and then the cheaper wine after the guests have had too much to drink; but you have saved the best till now" (verse 10, NIV).

This was the good stuff: 908 bottles of the best wine in the hood. Jesus was ridiculous and extravagant in His giving. It doesn't even make *sense*.

But, my friend, this is how to human. This is how we are supposed to give: above and beyond. And that's why when people see this sort of love in action, it changes their entire lives—not because of the gift, but because of seeing the giver give. It's a whole vibe.

• • •

An hour later, I looked down at my phone. Pope's vet bills were covered.

• • •

Three hours later, I looked at my phone again. Our basement flood damage had been provided for.

• • •

Five hours later, our cars had been paid off.

• • •

Eight hours later, Heather's hospital visit had been taken care of.

• • •

Twelve hours? Those twenty-one days at Vanderbilt Children's Hospital in 2019 had been paid for.

• • •

Twenty-four hours later, we were completely debt free. Every single piece of debt we owed besides our mortgage was gone. All of it. Gone.

Water into wine.

• • •

The good stuff. This wasn't the cheap hooch; this was the good stuff. Right before our eyes, we watched humans become not only the hands and feet of Jesus but also living miracles. Abundance. Gifts. To say I was humbled wouldn't begin to express it.

"Sharon, I don't even know what to say."

"You don't have to say anything, friend. You deserve this. You are loved."

I called Pastor Alex back and told her exactly how much money was given to us.

"Remember how you asked if you were cursed, Carlos?" she said. "Well, I'll take that curse any day!" We died laughing. It felt so good.

That love felt like freedom.

. . .

When Heather was released the next day, I was ready to fly back to Nashville.

"We're going to Denver," she said. "I have pain meds. Let's go to the snow."

When we put our heads down on our pillows that night, two things were true:

1. Our lives still were affected by the pain we had endured. My daughter's car was still in the shop. Our house was still flooded. Our dog was still gone. Our chickens were still dead. We still had rescued a murderous owl. Heather's wrist was still broken.

2. My faith in humanity had been restored. Seriously. I didn't think this was ever gonna be the case again after all that I had seen in my DMs over the past year. After all of the drama that I wanted to save for my mama but instead took

to sleep with me every single night. I didn't know if I would ever feel this feeling again. That we were all together. That we could pull this human thing off.

Nobody asked me who I voted for before they gave. Nobody asked me my thoughts on masks before they gave. They simply gave. And when they gave, I shut down my pride and I received. And when I received, I found myself finally free.

You see, this ridiculous generosity thing? It not only frees someone else, but it frees you. Something unlocked in my heart that night, and I wasn't going to throw away the key. I just didn't know who I was gonna give it to next, nor did I know how much they would need it too.

. . .

We are almost there, fam. We've got the key to set people free. When we give extravagantly, we free more rapidly. And what I love about this principle is that it doesn't mean we are all giving the same amount. Extravagance for one person is completely different than extravagance for another. There isn't a spreadsheet that will tell you what extravagance is for you. You can't plug your yearly income into a spreadsheet and have it spit out a number. You can't plug in the number of hours you have free and have an equation tell you how many hours you are supposed to volunteer in order for it to be considered extravagant. No. This is something that you are gonna have to feel in your gut. This is up to you. You will know. You will. Like I said early in this book, you must risk in order to rescue. Extravagance is risky business. But isn't that exactly how we are supposed to love other people? Extravagantly? Yes! That's the ticket. You will know what extravagance is when you give it, and you will know what it is when you don't. I wish I could give you a clever line that will help you figure it out, but you know what it is for you. What are you having to sacrifice in order to pull it off? What extravagance is going to help free someone today?

Now let's FREE HUMANS.

19

. . .

free empathy

How does one recover from a week like that, culminating in such lavish, humbling generosity? Talk about whiplash.

Over those next few weeks, I woke up every single day with the feeling that I still needed to pinch myself, wondering if all of it had been a strange dream. But it hadn't. People had really done this. *Strangers* had done this, out of nowhere. People who had no idea who I was or what I do or why I do what I do gave simply because someone they loved told them that someone else could use some money. It was all just too much.

What had led them to such human and kind acts of generosity? Conviction is one thing, but action is something entirely different. As I thought about it, I began to believe that the bridge between conviction and action had been empathy.

Empathy.

When you read that word, what feelings come to mind? For most of us, empathy isn't something that we love to think about. It normally brings feelings of sadness, right? Because we think that empathy must mean we feel sad for someone.

And although that can be true, that is not all that empathy entails.

Sympathy is feeling bad *for* someone.

Empathy is feeling bad *with* someone.

And that is what moves the human needle. That is what brings freedom to so many people. That is why every single bit of debt I had to my name was paid off in a single act of over-whelming water-to-wine generosity. People tuned in to the worst week of one random stranger's life and they felt bad *with* me not just felt bad *for* me. Conviction turned to action. It moved them to give.

• • •

The more I thought about this, the more I thought that I wanted to see what my community could do in the same spirit. My Instagram community had recently grown from a few thousand incredibly compassionate human beings to a hundred thousand incredibly compassionate human beings. My friend Sharon's followers (I was one of them and still am) called their group the Governerds. And so then, I thought my people needed a name too. There was something about feeling as though your online community has an actual *name* that propels humans to action, so I put it out there. I asked my people to vote on three names.

1. Los Amigos. Get it? Los Amigos. I'm Los. You are my friends. Translated in Spanish "The Friends" *and* "Los's Friends." Catchy, I know. That was my personal fav.
2. Hope Dealers. This is what a lot of my community would call themselves and us.

3. Instafamilia. This is what I called us every time I would
    start a new story in the morning. I would always come on
    my phone and say something like "Good morning, Insta-
    familia!" Get it? My Instagram familia. Listen, I'm not
    some marketing genius, but this just stuck. At the end of
    the voting, Instafamilia reigned supreme.

We were the Instafamilia. People started getting into it. I
started seeing hashtags all around the Insta-universe tagging
us and referencing conversations we were having about race
and such. I also know that the Instafamilia was a super-
diverse group. Every type of person seemed to be represented,
from all over the country and beyond. About half of them
lean left politically, and about half of them lean right politically. They pride themselves in being part of such a diverse
community.

*I wonder if this crew could come together and change someone's
life?* I would wonder over and over. I was convinced that our
common thread of empathy could be (and would be) the thing
that unified us. Then we got a chance to try.

Later that year, I got a DM sharing an account of a young
Black mother and wife who was recently diagnosed with epilepsy. She was having hundreds of seizures a day. Three
months prior, she had been completely healthy. Now her life
had been turned upside down. She had been trying for a few
months to raise enough money for a seizure-alert dog. This
dog would alert her before she had a seizure so that she could
get to a safe place. She had raised nine thousand dollars of her
twenty-five-thousand-dollar goal.

"I wonder if the Instafamilia could get her closer to the
goal," I said to Heather. And then I decided, *Nah, I don't want*

to ask people and then only a hundred dollars come in. That would
be embarrassing.

I see now how my own pride was getting in the way of just showing up and possibly blessing this woman. My ego was getting in the way of love. *So what if it is only a hundred dollars?* I thought. *That's a hundred more than she has now.* It was a Sunday afternoon. People aren't on their phones as much on the weekends. Another excuse.

As I thought about it, I felt a swell of confidence. We needed to do this. I had been sitting on the sofa, so I got up and walked to my front porch. I opened my camera and started talking. I asked the Instafamilia to try to help the woman get to her twenty-five-thousand-dollar goal. She had raised nine thousand dollars in two months. Maybe in a day we could get her a few more thousand. What did we think? I hit Send and felt like I had gotten it off my chest.

I had linked her GoFundMe page and didn't think about it for another hour until my phone started buzzing like crazy. I noticed that Shannell, the woman with epilepsy, had tagged me in a few videos. *That was kind,* I thought. *I wonder how it's going.* So, before I clicked to watch what she had said, I went over to her GoFundMe page. My jaw dropped.

Twenty-seven thousand dollars.

In one hour, the Instafamilia had blown her goal out of the water. What in the world?

And then I linked her Venmo. And in the following twenty-three hours, the Instafamilia gave more than forty thousand dollars to Shannell.

What in the world was this community? Who are these insane givers? My next post was something along these lines: "Um, hey, guys. What in the world just happened? Did you guys just give away that much money in less than twenty-four hours?" I was crying. (I cry a lot, if you haven't picked that up by now.)

I immediately started getting more and more DMs. People—lots of people—were asking me different versions of the same question: "When are we going to do that again? That was amazing!" People saw how their small gifts had stacked up to become something incredible. And the thing that got them going was their empathy. Empathy changed Shannell's life. They felt with her, so they gave to her.

. . .

This is how we do it, my friend. This is how we get people who don't look like us, vote like us, think like us, and so on to stand shoulder to shoulder with us.

Now, I'm not saying that this is a perfect or foolproof recipe. Being more human isn't a science. There will, of course, be things that some people will not be moved with empathy toward. But I do believe that empathy is the last great unifier. I believe that the more empathy humanity grows in, the more this world will come together.

Empathy is necessary. It's not optional for us to pull this human thing off. I'm gonna share another mind-blowing story of empathy in action in just a second, but let's pause and learn from the one we have been learning from all along: Jesus.

As we have seen in every chapter, Jesus is the human we need to take all cues from. The only reason I have been able to experience any of these human healing moments is that I have been looking at the life of Jesus and copying and pasting it into mine. Here is another copy-and-paste moment where we will see just how important empathy is to Jesus.

Let's head over to John 11. This is the chapter in the Bible with the shortest verse in the Bible. It's just two words: "Jesus wept" (verse 35).

That's the one. That's the verse that is going to show us exactly how important it is to have empathy in our lives. I'm no Greek scholar, I can't read Hebrew, I didn't go to seminary, but I'd like to offer my translation of this verse to you. I'd like to offer my scholarly translation. Here is it . . .

"Jesus had empathy."

You might be thinking, *Wait, Carlos, that is not what the original language says! The original Greek is just translated, "To shed tears." That says nothing of this New Age empathy you are trying to place on Jesus.*

But let's look at the rest of the text for a hot second:

A man was sick, Lazarus, from Bethany, the village of Mary and her sister Martha. Mary was the one who anointed the Lord with fragrant oil and wiped His feet with her hair, and it was her brother Lazarus who was sick. So the sisters sent a message to Him: "Lord, the one You love is sick."

When Jesus heard it, He said, "This sickness will not end in death but is for the glory of God, so that the Son of God may be glorified through it." Now Jesus loved Martha, her sister, and Lazarus. So when He heard that he was sick, He stayed two more days in the place where He was. Then after that, He said to the disciples, "Let's go to Judea again." (verses 1–7)

Okay, so what do we have here? We've got Jesus—like, *the* Jesus—getting word that two of His favorite humans, Mary and Martha, were worried that their sick brother was gonna die. And what I find peculiar is that Jesus didn't pack up and go there the moment He heard the news. No, He and His disciples hung out for a few more days. Then after those two days, He's like, *Aight, let's go.*

When Jesus arrived, He found that Lazarus had already been in the tomb four days. Bethany was near Jerusalem (about two miles away). Many of the Jews had come to Martha and Mary to comfort them about their brother. As soon as Martha heard that Jesus was coming, she went to meet Him. But Mary remained seated in the house.

Then Martha said to Jesus, "Lord, if You had been here, my brother wouldn't have died. Yet even now I know that whatever You ask from God, God will give You." (verses 17–22)

So, now Jesus has shown up and He is getting pressed by the sisters that if He just would not have taken so long, Lazarus would not had died. Jesus, You turn water into the *good wine.* We know You could have saved Lazarus. And Jesus absolutely knows He could have saved Lazarus. So why didn't He do it? I have a feeling you know where I'm going. If you don't, keep reading:

"Your brother will rise again," Jesus told her.

Martha said, "I know that he will rise again in the resurrection at the last day." (verses 23–24)

Again, Martha ain't getting it. Jesus wanted to turn that too-late rescue into an early resurrection. But that wasn't in Mary and Martha's plan.

When Mary came to where Jesus was and saw Him, she fell at His feet and told Him, "Lord, if You had been here, my brother would not have died!"

When Jesus saw her crying, and the Jews who had come with her crying, He was angry in His spirit and deeply moved. "Where have you put him?" He asked.

"Lord," they told Him, "come and see."

Jesus wept.

So the Jews said, "See how He loved him!"

(verses 32–36)

There it is.

Jesus knew He was gonna raise Lazarus from the dead. So why in the world did He weep? Why in the world did He expel emotion from His eyeballs when He knew the outcome? It's because of empathy.

You see, Jesus wasn't weeping because He was sad that Lazarus was dead. No, Jesus was sad because Mary and Martha were sad.

Jesus wept for them, not for Lazarus.

Jesus had *empathy.*

Jesus knew that in a matter of minutes, Lazarus was gonna come dancing out of that grave. He would have had every right to look at those mourning and roll His eyes, because their pain was gonna last for only a few more minutes. It was so temporary.

But Jesus didn't give those who mourned a speech to try to talk them out of their grief. He didn't give them data that proved they were really grieving for no reason. He didn't make them feel small for their lack of faith.

Jesus simply saw people hurting, and it made Him hurt as

well. He empathized so much with those who mourned that it made Him weep.

. . .

This is empathy to a T. This is why it is so important that even if we know better, even if we know that something is going to turn out better for those who are weeping, even if we initially feel silly for feeling sad with someone, we should still step into empathy. Empathy builds trust with those we are feeling with.

It's never been the money that has been the thing that has changed people in all the years of raising money for people. At the point of this writing, the Instafamilia has raised almost a million dollars for people. This is not a drill. One freaking million dollars.

We have raised $280,000 for a nonprofit called Brooklyn to Alaska so that they can build a base camp for the Black and Brown youth who are training to be river guides in Alaska.

We have raised $250,000 for kids who lost their homes to a wildfire in Northern California.

We raised $120,000 for my former guitar player who was sick in the hospital.

We raised another $120,000 for a woman who lost her husband and baby in the same week.

The Instafamilia don't play.

That's a big deal. We've seen huge things happen. Lavish water-to-wine generosity. Incredible weeping-by-the-tomb connections. And it's all been because of empathy.

Every single time I forward that money to the recipient, they say the same thing: "I don't feel worthy."

I get it. I know that feeling exactly. I mean, who *would* feel worthy? But it's not just about the money. Let me show you what I mean.

. . .

Recently, I was on my way home from a speaking event that had gotten canceled. I was bummed. I make my living off speaking events, so this was a gut punch in a month where Covid was spiking and events were canceling.

As I was sitting in the airport waiting for my next flight, I heard someone playing the piano, so I walked over to this man and watched him. He was going for it. He was all in. And I noticed something else: Nobody was paying attention to him. Everyone sitting around him was on their phones and not even batting an eye at his skills. He also had about twenty bucks in his tip jar.

And then it hit me: *He needs to be seen. He simply needs to be seen.*

So I pulled up a chair next to him and started paying closer attention than maybe anyone in the airport had in quite some time. He stopped playing and looked at me. "What's your name, young man?" he asked me. We ended up talking for about ten minutes. I learned his name was Tonee and that he had been on kidney dialysis for nine years. Every night for twelve hours, he goes through dialysis.

He was just so grateful to have been seen.

And then I had an idea. "Tonee, what's the biggest tip you have ever gotten?"

"Six hundred dollars," he replied, and then he went back to his piano.

I opened Instagram and told the Instafamilia it was time

once again to do their thing. I had thirty minutes before my next flight. "Let's see how big of a tip we can give Tonee before I take off."

Thirty minutes and ten thousand dollars later, I told Tonee about his tip.

The look on his face. The jaw dropping. The utter disbelief. "Who gave me ten thousand dollars?" he shouted.

"Eighty thousand people who love you and don't even know you," I replied.

After some tears, he looked me square in the eye and said, "My faith in humanity has been restored." He had been seen.

By the end of the day, Tonee had received more than sixty thousand dollars in tips. And the crazy part? Almost all that money? He gave it away. Because empathy isn't just about us freeing other humans. It's about them in turn freeing humans because they have been given freedom.

You see, this empathy thing—it's addictive. And I believe that the more we can find it inside us, the more that people around us will find it inside them. And then it's a domino effect of people all around us freeing others. That's called revival.

And it starts with a single person feeling *with* someone else.

• • •

Can you imagine if every single person reading this decided that today was gonna be the day they practiced radical empathy that turned into radical action that frees people?

Here's an important question to ask ourselves: Why is empathy so hard? Because it is. Empathy makes us uncomfortable, because feeling bad *with* someone is a lot harder than feeling bad *for* someone. With one you are connected; with the other you are watching.

One version of ourselves that is really bad at empathy is who I like to call the Dodger. This is someone who changes the subject or flees the conversation so fast in order to protect themselves from having to feel bad. You all know if you are this person or have seen someone become this person in an awkward moment. "How's it going, Lacy?" "Oh, it's going horribly. I just got diagnosed with cancer and I also lost my job." "Oh, wow. That's terrible. Um, man, I'm sorry. Hey, I gotta run. See ya!" They get out of the situation as fast as possible in order to reduce the amount of pain they feel. (Ever had a convo with one of those people? Yeah, that's kinda the worst.)

How about this next type of person? I like to call them the Positive Picker-Upper. (And this would be Carlos.) "Hey, how's it going?" "Oh, it's going horribly. I just got diagnosed with cancer and I also lost my job." "Oh, man! What kind of cancer? You know, there's so much better treatment these days! Also, what a great time to lose your job! We are in a great job market!" Yup. That's annoying (and also blatant attempts not to have to sit in the pain of the person suffering). Is that you? 'Cause it's me.

And the last version of empathy avoider is what I like to call the Advisor. This is the person who avoids empathy by giving advice. "Hey, how's it going?" "Oh, it's going horribly. I just got diagnosed with cancer and I also lost my job." "Really? Tell me what kind of cancer. Let me help you figure out how to get the best treatment. And about your job? Are you on Jobzilla.com? Have you applied to four companies a day? Because data suggests that this is how many applications you need to file in order for you to actually move the needle forward in the job market."

Yeah. Don't be that guy or gal. Don't be any of these three. All of these are simply ways to avoid empathy. Empathy, as it turns out, is more than sympathy. We need to get better at feeling *with* instead of feeling *for*. We need to ask why we are moving away from people in their pain. We need to listen more. To be quiet and learn to *be* with those who are suffering. We need to be more like Jesus, because when we avoid empathy, we miss a chance to return to a more human way of being. A more real, connected, *good* way of being. This is the good stuff. This is—moment by moment, relationship by relationship—how we human.

* * *

how to human

Did you know that destroying something is much easier than building something? It's oddly more satisfying to watch something get destroyed than to be built. It's why our mouths open slightly in awe when we watch a building collapse during a demolition but tend to open in a yawn for the months or years that building was under construction. To see the sheer, quick force of destruction is appealing to our human nature. It's just really impressive to watch things suddenly shudder and fall.

Building something is not nearly as enjoyable as watching it collapse. It takes a lot more work. It takes a lot more conversation. It takes a lot more planning. But if we do it right, then at the end of all the work, planning, and conversation, there will sit something we can be proud of. Something for generations to come.

That's why it's important to make sure to recognize what you are getting good at. Are you getting better at being a demolitionist or a constructionist? Are you listening to more voices that are calling for you to destroy things or to build things? It's so *easy* to destroy things. Any person could destroy a building with a single match and little well-placed gasoline. But could the same person build that building? Of course not. It's so much harder.

· · ·

In order for us to be more human, I'm asking us all to be builders. The world is overrun with demolitionists. These are the people bringing things down—cutting with their words, razing lives with their actions, dismissing or mocking or insulting their neighbors, living like only they matter—and letting others pick up the pieces. But destroying stuff is an easy job. You want a real challenge? Something worthy of your uniqueness and skills? Be a builder instead.

See a problem? Build a solution. See a need? Build a solution.

We need more people willing to play the long game of building instead of getting the quick hit of dopamine that destruction gives us. Sure, there are times to destroy things. But dare I say that there should be more times to build things, lest we end up with nothing but rubble?

I want to split the readers of this book in two for a second, and not to pit sides against each other. More so that we can all see what the goal at hand is. First, I want to talk to those of you who may not think Jesus is who He claimed to be. Those of you who think He was simply a really good dude. A really good human. The whole point of how I wrote this book was intended to draw you in, not to alienate you. Even if you do not believe in Jesus the way I believe in Him, you can still learn all these amazing and incredible life hacks from His life. Like, take the whole God thing out of it and He still wins the human award. Mother Teresa, Gandhi, the pope, and all the other incredible humans who have walked the face of the earth all had very impactful lives, but none of them have had the impact Jesus did. So that's why I felt completely comfortable teaching on the life of Jesus without the supernatural aspect of it. Because although I believe in the supernatural aspect of it—that He is God made flesh—you don't have to in order to learn and live the message of this book.

So, I would ask you to consider diving deeper into His life by reading the Bible. It's a "how to human" manual way better suited for quoting than my words. Like LeVar Burton used to say on *Reading Rainbow,* "You don't have to take *my* word for it." No. Grab yourself a Bible. Read it for yourself. Start with the gospel of John. Nothing else for now.* Just read about the life of Jesus in this account written by one of His closest friends. Then copy and paste. Pick up the love you see and put it in your life.

Read about Jesus. Copy and paste. Do that over and over again and watch those around you begin to be influenced by the way you live. Watch people around you begin to feel safer. Watch people around you begin to feel as if they are a little more human too as you are honest like Jesus, selfless like Jesus. As you listen like Jesus. As you notice those other people overlook like Jesus. Later on, one of the great early Christians, Paul, would describe how a life in the Spirit of Jesus looks:

The fruit of the Spirit is love, joy, peace, forbearance, kindness, goodness, faithfulness, gentleness and self-control.

---

* If you want some dessert after the main meal, I would say read the books of First and Second John as well. I know that is a lot of John. But trust me— John had it going on.

Against such things there is no law. (Galatians 5:22–23, NIV)

Those things, fam. *Those things.* Ask yourself every single day if those are the attributes that are pouring out of your life. I promise you will be better for it. What would it be like to live in a world where these qualities were what we were known for?

And the message here? *You matter.* So much. So MUCH. You have *so much* to offer the world. And the version of yourself that aligns itself most with the way Jesus lived is going to not only bring the best out of your humanity but also bring the best out of those around you. I'm in this too. I'm proud to link arms with you. I see you in my Instagram DMs on a daily basis. You are kindness. You are love. You are hope. I am so grateful to be on this journey of hope-dealing with you and am grateful you trust this crazy Jesus-loving, Bible-believing person with so much of your heart. I will never take it for granted. You have the potential to change the world, one heart at a time.

Now I want to talk to the Christians for a second, only because if you call yourself a Christian, that means you believe some weird stuff. Stuff like the fact that Jesus wasn't just a man but that He is God too. Stuff like that He was murdered and then after being dead a few days got up again. Stuff like that you can talk to Him and He will talk back to you. See what I mean? That is some crazy stuff. And I wholeheartedly believe all that. That makes *me* crazy too.

And since we are here together in this craziness, I want to press you a little bit harder for a second, because I think that for the past few years, Christians in our culture (at least most of the loud ones) have been getting it wrong. People who have been calling themselves Christians have become some of the most hateful and rage-filled humans on planet Earth, particularly on social media and in the news. And when I look at the life of Jesus, I do not think there is a lot of copy and paste going on in the lives of many of us who claim to follow Him. I don't think there is a lot of looking at Jesus going on. Not nearly as much as looking at our own opinions, politics, or comfort.

But I want to do better. And I want you to do better with me. Because I'm a follower of Jesus, it's my responsibility to ferociously pour His love on my friends *and* my foes. It's not my responsibility to convict them. That is the role of the Holy Spirit. Comment-section debates won't convince a heart to change. Thirty-second video clips where your side "destroys" the other team won't convince a heart to change. Those may make *us* feel better but won't ever move their hearts toward change. So, is that love? Does it bring joy? Encourage peace? Go through that list of the fruit of the Spirit from Galatians and compare it to how we so often *are*. Does it line up? Probably not. Not like it should.

We must love those we disagree with in order to let them know they matter. That they are seen. That's the actual goal. That's what will move a heart toward seeing things differently. That's what will help us all human better. That's why when you see a "Christian" online calling other humans names meant to wound them, it should make you cringe— even if you agree with their point of view. (And if it doesn't make you cringe, there are deeper problems.) Now, just because it's the Holy Spirit's role to convict doesn't mean we don't have convictions. It just means that when we take on

His role ourselves, with our human nature, it's far easier to fall into the trap of demeaning someone made in the image of God by throwing cheap and easy insults.

Woke Left. Basement Dweller. Snowflake. Trumpster. Deplorable. Libtard. Let's Go Brandon.

Those are just a few of the insults that make me cringe when I see a Jesus follower use them to jab someone who politically disagrees with them. I'm sure there will be new ones—and plenty of them—in the coming years. That's what happens when we try to play Holy Spirit. That's not our job. I've seen so many people come to the table of conversation with me by showing them I love them despite disagreeing with them. So as you continue to try to be Christlike in a divided and polarized world, start to pay attention to the voices you let into your head and heart. Nobody can pull this off perfectly. That's why we need the Holy Spirit. But I've yet to find anyone who has changed their mind on an important subject because they got "owned" or made to feel like an idiot in a conversation. Have you? So why do we all feel like that is the way forward together? What these sorts of online debates are changing are not minds but dopamine levels.

...

Managing a hard conversation or a difficult relationship isn't a science. But I'll tell you something that I've found true when I've shifted my thinking on an important subject matter: The person who helped me shift never made me feel small. Minds change when they are made to feel large. When they are respected and gently challenged. When they are helped to stretch and make more room for another point of view. And as we think about all this, about how to be in the world, about how to see and free in the world, what really matters most is also what is most simple: *showing up and loving.*

So as you stand up for what you believe in, build up those who disagree with you instead of tearing them down. Then watch their capacity to understand increase, right along with yours. We are called as Christians and, dare I say, as *humans* to wake up every day with one goal: to love others ferociously. *All* others. As we learn to do this, we will watch their hearts open up to change much faster than sharp words or clever comebacks could ever do.

That's it. That's the secret sauce: love. We all don't have to agree on everything, but we can decide not to let our natural and sincere disagreements turn us into angry, rage-filled humans.

There is so much more out there for you. Don't spend all your waking hours trying to destroy some "other side." 'Cause when the end of your days finally comes, your friends and family are gonna wanna talk about how hard you loved, not how hard you hated.

You see, we *need* each other. All of us. We were created with each other in mind. I believe there was a design set forth for humanity to live in harmony. Not totally without conflict, but with *harmony* being the goal. And just think about that for a minute. You know that in a song there can be no harmony without a melody. The melody is what carries the song. The melody is what people remember when they are singing back a song. But you know what the harmony does? The harmony makes the song explode. The harmony makes the hair on the back of your neck stand up. The harmony is what makes people pay attention. A song can be sung without harmony, but the harmony puts it over the top. Harmony can happen only when we each sing our unique part. It doesn't happen in spite of differences; it happens *because* of them. Let's not try to be just a catchy melody; let's live as the symphony of humanity we were created to be. That's only possible *together*.

What do you say? Are we ready to right this ship? Let's take these lessons we have learned and begin writing the next season of humanity. You know we have that ability. We do. *You* do.

Now go. Right now. Into whatever craziness and challenge you have. Into whatever impossible situations you face. Into that tough relationship. Into that hard conversation. Into that opportunity to love. To help. To harmonize.

See humans.

Free humans.

And more than anything, as you live and love and post and play and work, just plain . . .

Be humans.

ABOUT THE AUTHOR

CARLOS WHITTAKER is bringing hope to humans all over the world. And he's pretty good at it. He's an author, podcaster, and global speaker backed by the power of a massive Instafamilia, his enthusiastic social media followers who tune in daily to join forces with him to find connection, do good, and be in community.

When Carlos enters a room, he makes people feel seen. His superpower is creating spaces—online and in person—where people are safe to engage in conversation about the topics that matter most to us but that we too often avoid. His motto? "Don't stand on issues. Walk with people."

All day every day, Carlos is a family man. He and his wife, Heather, live with their three amazing children in Nashville, Tennessee, where you can find them working on the family farm, planning trips around the world, and dancing to "Single Ladies (Put a Ring on It)" by Beyoncé (seriously, google it).

ABOUT THE TYPE

This book was set in Scala, a typeface designed by Martin Majoor in 1991. It was originally designed for a music company in the Netherlands and then was published by the international type house FSI FontShop. Its distinctive extended serifs add to the articulation of the letterforms to make it a very readable typeface.

Experience the Wild and Wonder Jesus Promises

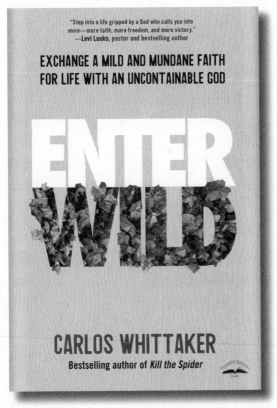

With his trademark blend of humor and transparency, Carlos Whittaker shares his personal struggle in coping with crippling anxiety—and how rediscovering a wild faith was the key to his freedom. That key can be yours, helping you open the door to leave mild and enter wild.

WATERBROOK

Learn more about Carlos's books at WaterBrookMultnomah.com

CARLOS WHITTAKER is a self-professed "hope dealer" who spends the majority of his time writing books and speaking on stages around the world. He is a People's Choice Award winner and author of several other books, including *Moment Maker, Kill the Spider*, and *Enter Wild*. He hosts the podcast *Human Hope*.

To learn more about Carlos and his work, subscribe to the podcast at **HumanHopePodcast.com**